FrontPage® 2000
fast&easy™

Send Us Your Comments

To comment on this book or any other PRIMA TECH title, visit our reader response page on the Web at **www.prima-tech.com/comments**.

How to Order

For information on quantity discounts, contact the publisher: Prima Publishing, P.O. Box 1260BK, Rocklin, CA 95677-1260; (916) 632-4400. On your letterhead, include information concerning the intended use of the books and the number of books you wish to purchase. For individual orders, visit PRIMA TECH's Web site at **www.prima-tech.com**.

FrontPage® 2000
fast&easy™

Coletta Witherspoon

A DIVISION OF PRIMA PUBLISHING

A Division of Prima Publishing

Prima Publishing and colophon are registered trademarks of Prima Communications, Inc. PRIMA TECH and Fast & Easy are trademarks of Prima Communications, Inc., Rocklin, California 95765.

Publisher: Stacy L. Hiquet

Associate Publisher: Nancy Stevenson

Managing Editor: Dan J. Foster

Senior Acquisitions Editor: Deborah F. Abshier

Project Editor: Kevin W. Ferns

Assistant Project Editor: Estelle Manticas

Technical Reviewer: Tim Altom

Copy Editor: Maria Paddock

Editorial Assistant: Brian Thomasson

Interior Layout: Shawn Morningstar

Cover Design: Prima Design Team

Indexer: Emily Glossbrenner

Microsoft, Windows, Windows NT, Outlook, MSN, and FrontPage are trademarks or registered trademarks of Microsoft Corporation.

Important: If you have problems installing or running Microsoft FrontPage, go to Microsoft's Web site at **www.microsoft.com**. Prima Publishing cannot provide software support.

Prima Publishing and the author have attempted throughout this book to distinguish proprietary trademarks from descriptive terms by following the capitalization style used by the manufacturer.

Information contained in this book has been obtained by Prima Publishing from sources believed to be reliable. However, because of the possibility of human or mechanical error by our sources, Prima Publishing, or others, the Publisher does not guarantee the accuracy, adequacy, or completeness of any information and is not responsible for any errors or omissions or the results obtained from the use of such information. Readers should be particularly aware of the fact that the Internet is an ever-changing entity. Some facts may have changed since this book went to press.

ISBN: 0-7615-1931-9

Library of Congress Catalog Card Number: 98-68144

Printed in the United States of America

01 02 03 DD 10 9 8 7 6 5 4

To Henry and Maisie

Acknowledgments

Many, many thanks to all the folks at Prima who have shown their support and confidence during each and every book we've worked on together. I'd like to thank Debbie Abshier for always keeping me busy. Kevin Ferns does a fantastic job of keeping everything on time and on track. I'd also like to thank Maria Paddock, Tim Altom, and Brian Thomasson for doing such a thorough job of checking over the manuscript.

About the Author

Coletta Witherspoon is a confirmed Web junkie. She was introduced to computers in the late 70s and began working as a technical writer in the environs of Redmond in the mid 80s. After a decade of suits and ties, she and her husband moved to a small farm in the middle of nowhere, converted the living room into an office, and now conduct all their business over the Internet. Coletta is the author of several *Fast & Easy* series books from PRIMA TECH.

Contents at a Glance

PART IV
ENHANCING YOUR WEB SITE 165

PART V
FINISHING YOUR WEB SITE 259

APPENDIXES 295

Contents

PART II
CREATING YOUR WEB SITE 33

Introduction

This *Fast & Easy* series book from Prima Tech will help you master FrontPage 2000 so that you can create informative and attractive Web sites. FrontPage is a versatile program for both experienced and beginning Web site designers looking to build sophisticated Web sites. FrontPage offers an array of creative tools for Web site design and management. Wizards and other dynamic options can help you develop fresh and exciting Web presentations. Whether you have an existing Web site that you want to improve or you are designing your first Web page, you will find the information you need in this book.

Who Should Read this Book?

This book is directed toward the novice computer user who needs a hands-on approach to Web page development. The generous use of illustrations makes this an ideal tool for those who have never used a Web site design program before. This book is also for those who are familiar with other Web site design programs and want to quickly apply their skills with FrontPage 2000.

This book is organized so you can quickly look up tasks to help you complete a job or learn a new trick. You may need to read an entire chapter to master a subject, or you may only need to refer to a certain section to refresh your memory.

Special Features of This Book

You'll notice that this book keeps explanations to a minimum to help you learn faster. You will find other features in this book that provide more information on how to work with FrontPage 2000:

- **Tips** offer helpful hints about features in FrontPage that can make your job a little easier and add spice to your Web pages.

- **Notes** offer additional information about FrontPage 2000 to enhance your learning experience with the new software.

Also, the appendixes show you how to install the FrontPage software and how to speed up your work with important keystroke shortcuts.

Happy designing!

PART I

Getting Familiar with FrontPage

1

Getting Started with FrontPage 2000

If you've never used FrontPage before, you may not know where to start. The program's interface and assortment of buttons and menus may overwhelm you. If so, this chapter will help clear things up a bit. In this chapter, you'll learn how to:

- Start FrontPage
- Execute commands with menus and toolbars
- View your Web page from different angles
- Understand the Page view
- Get help from within the program
- Exit FrontPage

Starting FrontPage

Before you can begin exploring FrontPage, you must first open the FrontPage program. It only takes a few mouse clicks to set you on your way.

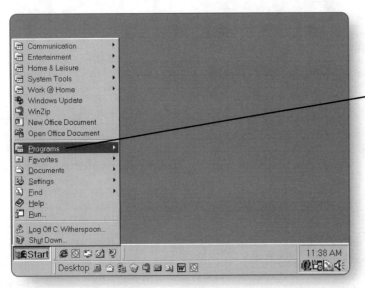

1. **Click** on the **Start button** on the Windows Taskbar. The Start menu will appear.

2. **Move** the **mouse pointer** to Programs. The Programs menu will appear.

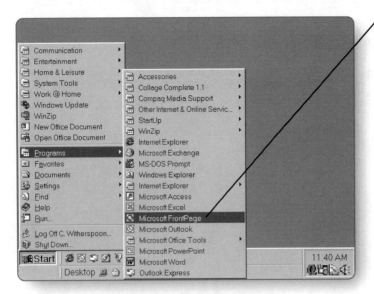

3. **Click** on **Microsoft FrontPage**. FrontPage will open.

Exploring FrontPage

When you look at the FrontPage screen, you'll notice an assortment of buttons, icons, menus, and scroll bars. These screen elements help you perform every task and function available in FrontPage. This section will show you the basics of working with the various FrontPage elements.

Using Menus

Menus contain all of the functions that a software program can perform. There are several menus located on a bar across the top of the FrontPage screen. Each menu includes a number of related commands.

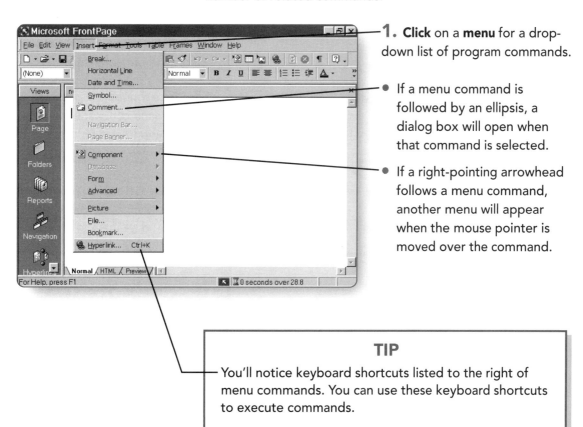

1. Click on a **menu** for a drop-down list of program commands.

- If a menu command is followed by an ellipsis, a dialog box will open when that command is selected.

- If a right-pointing arrowhead follows a menu command, another menu will appear when the mouse pointer is moved over the command.

TIP
You'll notice keyboard shortcuts listed to the right of menu commands. You can use these keyboard shortcuts to execute commands.

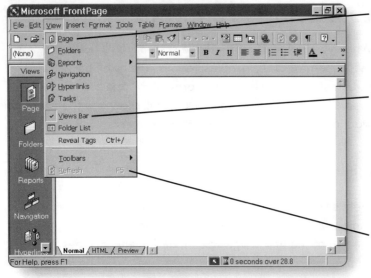

- When an icon next to a menu command is recessed, it means the function is displayed in the FrontPage window.

- When a menu command is preceded by a check mark, the command acts as a toggle. A check mark turns the function on; a missing check mark means the function is turned off.

- When a menu command is grayed out, it means the command is not available. You may need to perform some preliminary action to use the grayed-out command.

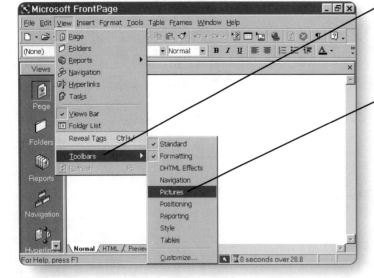

2. Place the **mouse pointer** over a menu command with a right-pointing arrowhead. A second menu will appear.

3. Move the **mouse pointer** to the right over a command on the second menu. The command will be highlighted.

NOTE

If you click on a menu command, that command will be executed or a dialog box will open and you will need to supply more information before the command can be executed.

Using Toolbars

The FrontPage toolbars display across the top of the program window and contain shortcut buttons for many menu commands.

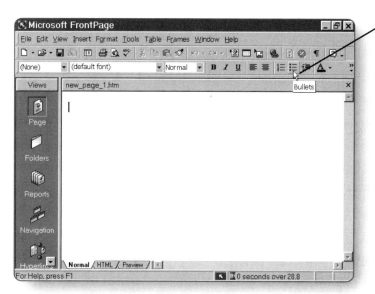

1. Place the **mouse pointer** over each toolbar button. A tool tip will appear telling you what function the button performs.

NOTE

Toolbar buttons are grouped into related functions, and a vertical line separates each group. This makes it easier to find what you need on the toolbar quickly.

Working with Dialog Boxes

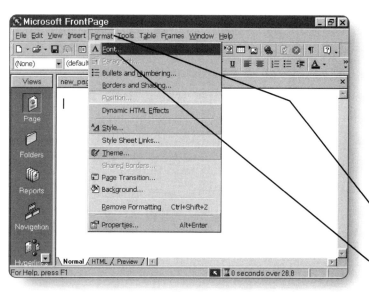

Dialog boxes group several related functions into one place. They allow you to select options and input specific information pertaining to the selected menu command. Before you work with the example in this section, be sure that you are using the Page view.

1. Click on **Format**. The Format menu will appear.

2. Click on **Font**. The Font dialog box will open.

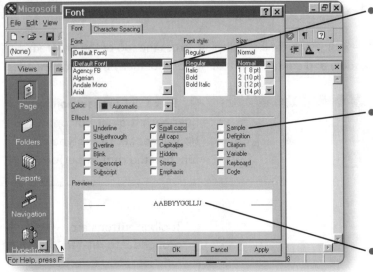

● Choose options by clicking on the arrow at either end of the vertical scroll bar to view the options, and then click on an option to select it.

● Turn options on and off by clicking on the check box to the left of the feature's name. A check mark in the check box means the feature is turned on. A blank check box mean the feature is turned off.

● View the effect of an option by looking at the display in the Preview pane.

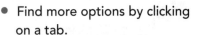

● Find more options by clicking on a tab.

● Select options from drop-down lists by clicking on the down arrow.

● Adjust numbers and measurements by clicking on the up and down arrows.

NOTE

Click on Cancel if you don't want to alter the font or apply new settings at this time.

---

3. Click on **OK**. The dialog box will close and the options will be applied to the Web page.

Moving around with Scroll Bars

You'll find two types of scroll bars in FrontPage: vertical scroll bars and horizontal scroll bars. Both forms work the same way, except that the horizontal scroll bar moves you across the page while the vertical bar allows you to move up and down on the page. You'll begin creating pages such as the one shown in Chapter 3, "Designing a Web Site."

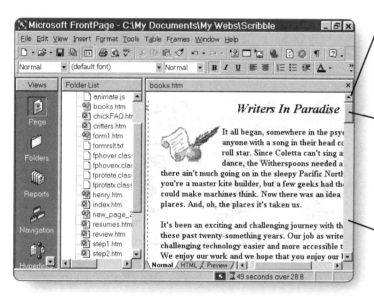

1. **Click** on the **arrow** at either end of the vertical scroll bar. The page will shift up or down one line at a time.

2. **Press and hold** the **mouse button** on the scroll box and **drag** it **up or down** within the scroll bar. The page will shift up or down accordingly.

3. **Click** inside the **scroll bar**. The page will shift up or down one screen at a time.

Understanding the Views Bar

FrontPage helps you create and manage a Web site. The Views Bar contains several features to help you organize your Web site's structure, move files and folders, add and delete pages and files, view the relationship between hyperlinks, and create tasks and reports to make your job of creating a Web site a little easier.

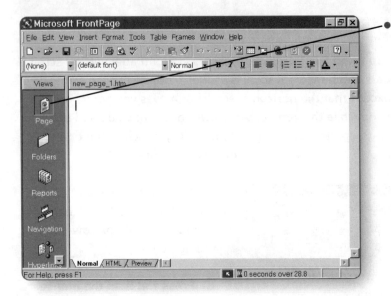

- The Page view is where you'll create each individual Web page. You have three different options for creating and viewing each page within the standard Page view. These options will be discussed later in this chapter.

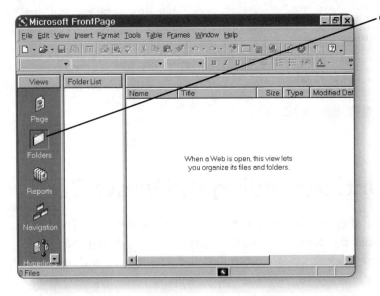

- The Folders view shows the arrangement of your Web page elements into folders and subfolders. This view looks very much like the screen in Windows Explorer.

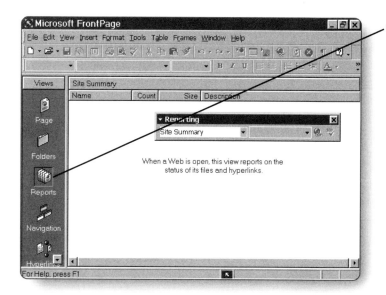

● The Reports view displays a list of reports that you can create to help you keep your Web site up to date.

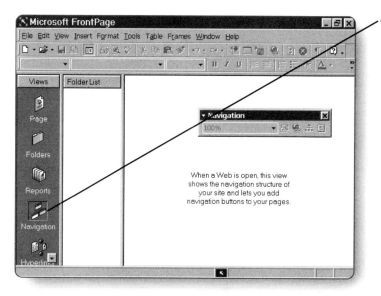

● The Navigation view displays an organization chart of your Web site.

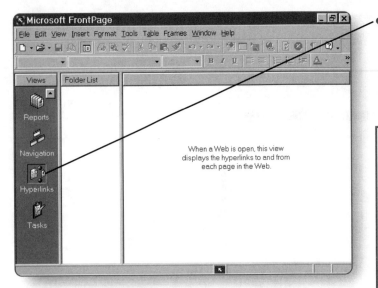

● The Hyperlinks view shows a diagram of links between the pages within your Web site, and of links to Web sites outside your Web site.

NOTE

If you don't see a particular Views button on your screen, click on the down arrow at the bottom right of the Views bar. The list of Views buttons will scroll down. An up arrow button will appear at the top right of the Views bar.

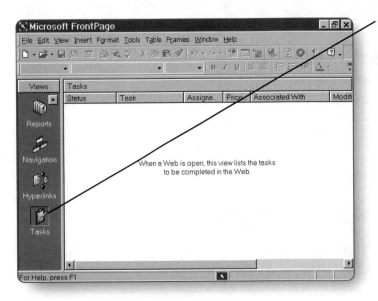

● The Tasks view shows which parts of your Web site have tasks assigned to them and the status of those tasks.

Looking at the Page Layout Views

The Page view is where most of your Web page designing and editing will take place. The Page view displays text, graphics, and other page elements in one of three formats: Normal WYSIWYG (What You See Is What You Get), HTML, or preview format.

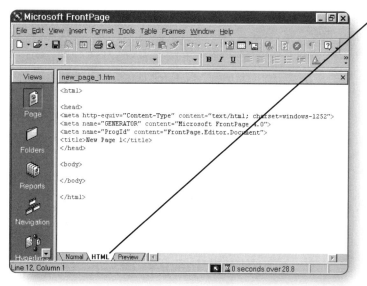

● You will do most of your Web page creation in the Normal Page view. This is where you will design and lay out your Web pages. In this view, you can place text, graphics, and other Web page elements where you want them to appear in the final product. Use the toolbars and menus to format and position your page elements.

● If you know how to create HTML code, you can use the HTML view to insert the HTML.

NOTE

If you are interested in learning more about using HTML, check out PRIMA TECH's *Learn HTML In a Weekend, Revised Edition.*

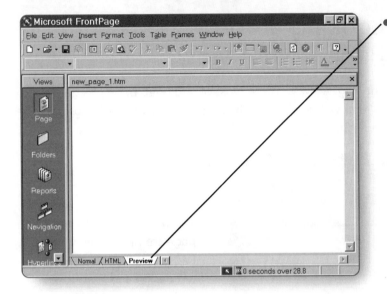

● The Preview Page view lets you view your Web page in a browser window. This is not actually a browser, but it will give you the same feeling. You can click on hyperlinks to see where they will take you, and you can see how some of your animations and dynamic effects will display in a browser.

Getting Help

If you are unfamiliar with a feature or function of FrontPage, there are a couple of places where you can get help.

Searching the Help Topics

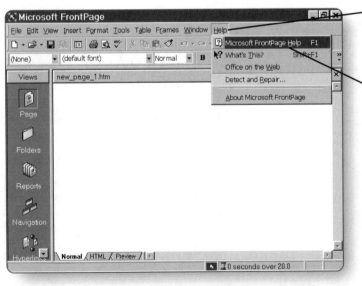

1. Click on **Help** on the menu toolbar. The Help menu will appear.

2. Click on **Microsoft FrontPage Help**. The Help system will show the Help topics with the Contents tab displayed.

NOTE

To make the Help window larger, click on the Maximize button.

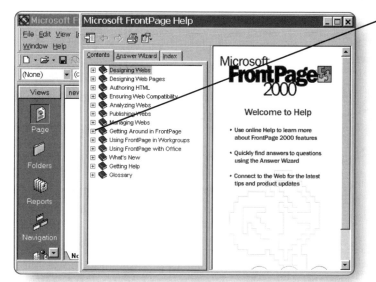

3. **Click** on the **plus sign** to the left of the topic you want to know more about. The topic will expand to show the contents.

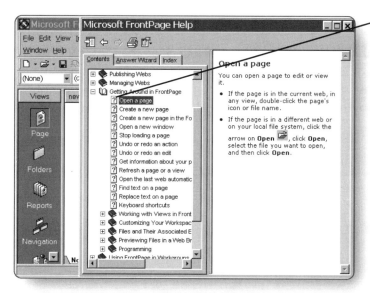

4. **Click** on the **topic** about which you need more information. The associated help file will appear in the right side of the Help window.

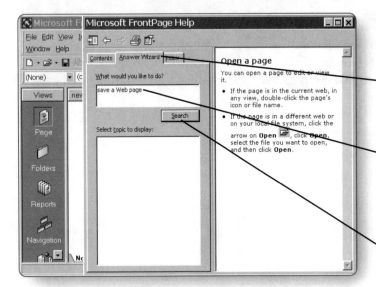

Getting Help from the Answer Wizard

1. **Click** on the **Answer Wizard tab**. The Answer Wizard will appear.

2. **Type** a few **words** to describe the task with which you need help in the What would you like to do? text box.

3. **Click** on the **Search button**. A list of possible help topics will appear in the Select Topic to display list box.

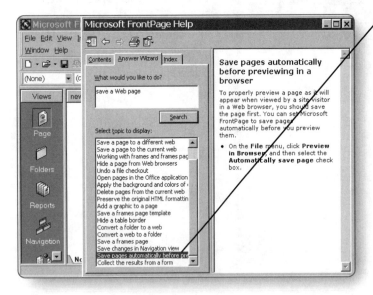

4. **Click** on the **topic** that you want to read. The associated Help file will appear in the right side of the Help window.

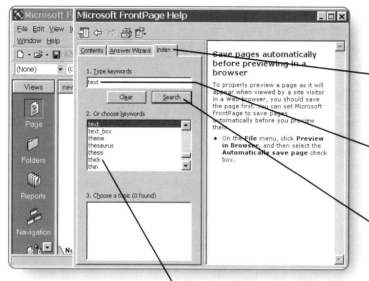

Searching the Help Index

1. Click on the **Index tab**. The Index tab will come to the top of the stack.

2. Type a **keyword** in the Type keywords text box that describes the type of help you are seeking.

3. Click on the **Search button**. A list of Help topics will appear in the Choose a Topic list box.

TIP

You can also scroll through the Or choose keywords scroll box and select a topic from the list.

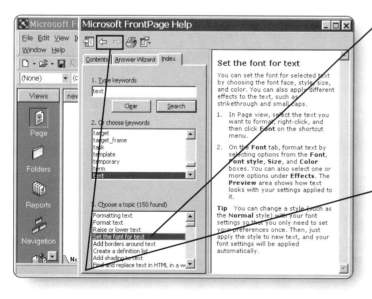

4. Click on a **topic** in the Choose a Topic list box that closely matches your request. The associated Help file will appear in the right side of the Help window.

TIP

Use the Back and Forward buttons to switch between Help topics that you've already viewed.

5. Click on the **Close button**. The Help window will close.

Using the Help Button

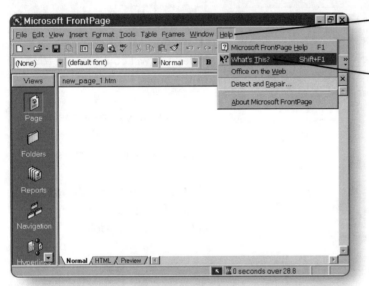

1. Click on **Help**. The Help menu will appear.

2. Click on **What's This?** The mouse pointer will change to a pointer with a question mark.

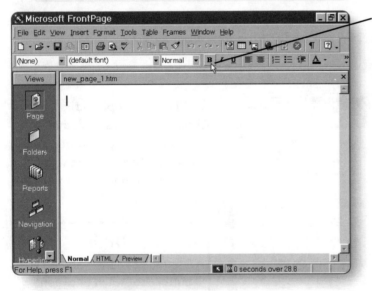

3. Click on the **item** about which you want more information. A Help window will display the Help file for that item.

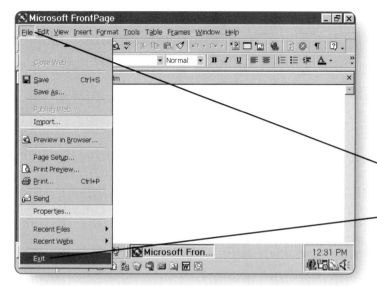

Exiting FrontPage

When you are finished working in FrontPage, you will need to close the program.

1. Click on **File**. The File menu will appear.

2. Click on **Exit**. FrontPage will close.

2

Customizing the FrontPage Screen

FrontPage has a fully customizable interface, which means you can change the way menus, toolbars, and commands appear inside the program window. All this promises to make your life easier (at least when you're working with FrontPage). You can move and hide toolbars to create more working space. You can make commands more readily available by placing them in convenient spots on toolbars. In this chapter, you'll learn how to:

- Add and delete buttons on a toolbar
- Play hide-and-seek with toolbars
- Reposition toolbars in the FrontPage window
- Customize the menu display
- Display the Views bar differently

Changing Toolbar Buttons

After you've worked with FrontPage for a while, you may find that you use some menu commands more frequently and want to place them on a toolbar. You can also remove buttons you use less frequently to create more space. After you become a Web pro, you can delete the Help button.

Adding Commands to Toolbars

1. **Right-click** on an **empty area** of the Menu bar or toolbar. A menu will appear.

2. **Click** on **Customize**. The Customize dialog box will open.

3. **Click** on the **Commands tab**. The Commands tab will come forward.

4. In the list of Categories, **select** the **menu** that contains the command you want to add to a toolbar. The menu will be highlighted, and the associated commands will be listed in the Commands box.

5. **Click and hold** the mouse button on the **command** that you want to add to a toolbar. The cursor will change to show that a button for the command can be placed on a toolbar.

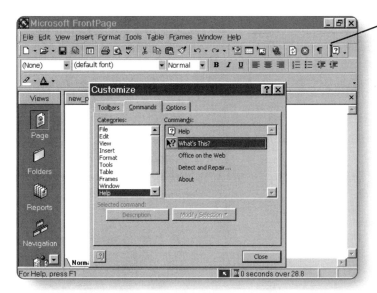

6. Drag the **mouse pointer** to the place on the toolbar where you want the command button to be located. A bar will appear in that location.

7. Release the **mouse button**. A button for the command will appear on the toolbar in the place you selected.

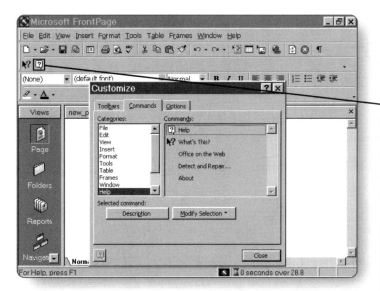

Deleting Commands from Toolbars

1. Press and hold the mouse pointer on the toolbar **button** that you want to remove from the toolbar. The mouse pointer will change to indicate that the button can be removed.

TIP

If you remove a button and later find that you want it back, you can add it from the Customize dialog box.

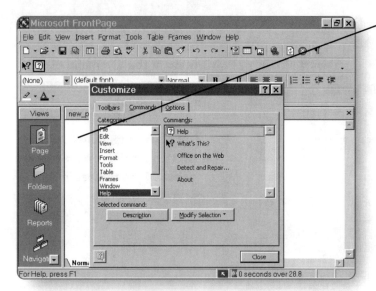

2. **Drag** the **mouse pointer** away from the toolbars. On the toolbar, the button will be surrounded by a black box indicating that it is about to be removed.

3. **Release** the **mouse button**. The toolbar button will be removed.

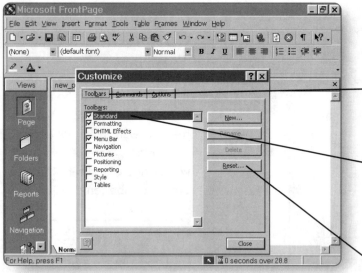

Restoring Toolbars to Their Original State

1. **Click** on the **Toolbars tab**. The Toolbars tab will come forward.

2. **Click** on the **toolbar** for which you want to restore default settings. The toolbar will be selected.

3. **Click** on the **Reset button**. A confirmation dialog box will appear.

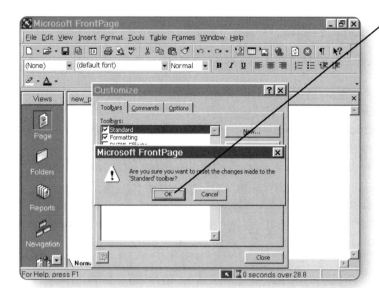

4. **Click** on **OK**. The toolbar will be reset to its default settings.

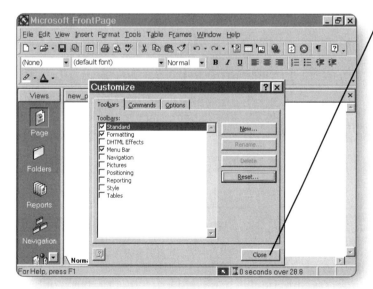

5. **Click** on **Close**. The Customize dialog box will close.

Adding and Removing Toolbars

FrontPage contains a number of toolbars that you can display at will. When you first open FrontPage, you'll notice the Standard and Formatting toolbars displayed at the top of your screen. These two toolbars are set as the default because most of your page editing tools are found there.

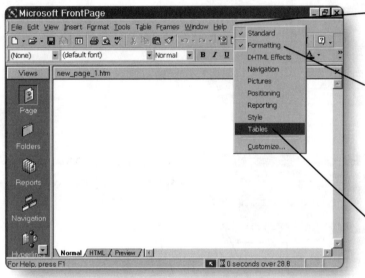

1. Right-click on an empty area of the **Menu bar or toolbar**. A menu will appear.

2a. To close a toolbar, **click** on a **toolbar** that has a check mark to the left of it. The toolbar will disappear from the FrontPage window.

OR

2b. To open a toolbar, **click** on a **toolbar** that does not have a check mark to the left of it. The toolbar will appear in a separate window.

NOTE

If you're uncertain about when or how to use these different toolbars, you'll find plenty of answers as you progress through this book and learn about FrontPage's many features.

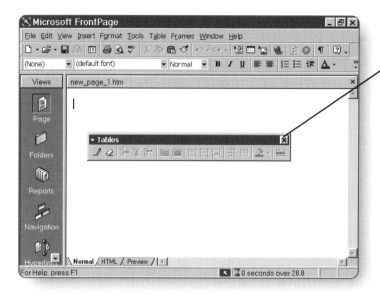

TIP

Close a toolbar window by clicking on the Close button.

Moving Toolbars

Place toolbars where they work best for you. Take some time and try several arrangements: move the toolbars around; place several toolbars on one line; let other toolbars float around your screen.

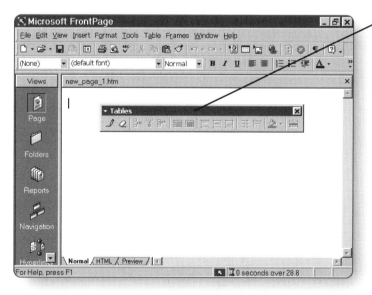

1. **Click and hold** the mouse button on the **title bar** of an open toolbar window.

2. **Move** the **mouse pointer** toward the Formatting toolbar. The toolbar will appear on the line below the Formatting toolbar.

TIP

To return the toolbar to a free-floating window, click and hold on the toolbar and drag it away from the other toolbars.

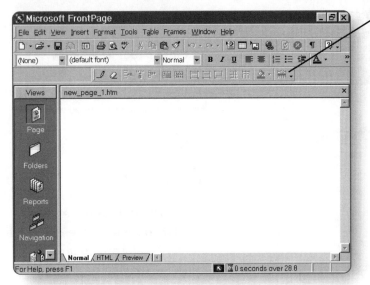

3. Click and hold the **mouse pointer** on the vertical bar at the left end of a toolbar. The mouse pointer will change to a four-sided arrow.

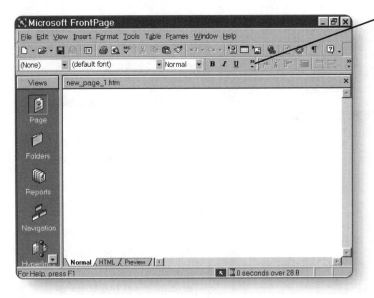

4. Move the **mouse pointer** to the same line as the Formatting toolbar. Both toolbars will appear on the same line.

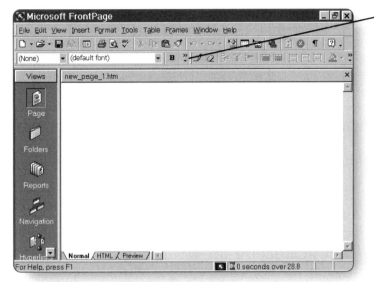

5. Press and hold the mouse button on the **vertical line** separating two toolbars and **move** the **mouse pointer** to the left or right. One toolbar will become longer and the other will become shorter.

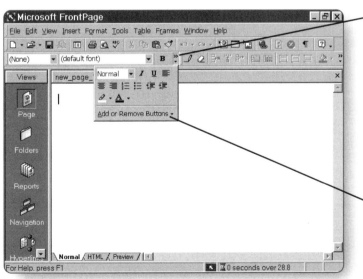

6. Click on the **double arrowhead** on the right end of a toolbar that is not completely displayed. Buttons that are hidden will appear in a drop-down list. Click on a button to execute the desired command.

TIP

You can also use the Add or Remove Buttons command to change the buttons that appear on the toolbar.

Customizing the Menu Display

You can change the way menus open by enabling one of the menu animations. You can also change how commands are listed when a menu is opened.

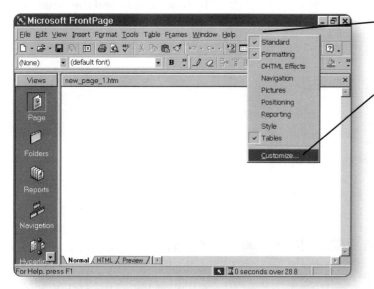

1. **Right-click** on an empty area of the **Menu bar or toolbar**. A menu will appear.

2. **Click** on **Customize**. The Customize dialog box will open.

3. **Click** on the **Options tab**. The Options tab will come forward.

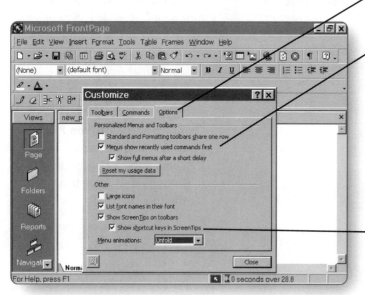

4. **Click** in the **check boxes** to specify which commands should display when the menu is opened and when the rest of the commands should appear. A check mark will appear in the chosen boxes.

TIP

To make it easier to learn keyboard shortcuts for toolbar commands, check the Show shortcut keys in ScreenTips check box.

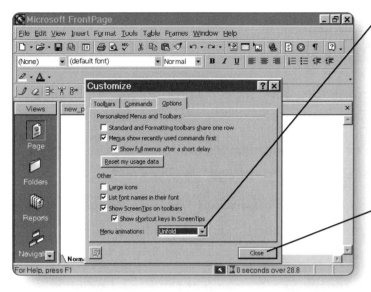

5. **Click** on the **down arrow** next to the Menu animations list box. A list of animations will appear.

6. **Click** on an **animation**. The animation will appear in the list box, and the menus will do a cute trick or two each time you open one.

7. **Click** on **Close**. Your new settings will be applied to the FrontPage menus.

Changing the Views Bar

You can change the Views Bar to make it easier to see all of the icons. You can also hide the Views Bar to give yourself more room for Web page creation. If you hide the Views Bar, you can always access the different views from the View menu on the menu bar at the top of the program window.

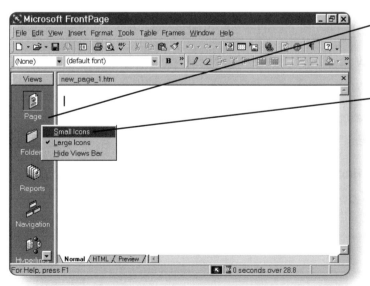

1. **Right click** on an empty area of the **Views Bar**. A menu will appear.

2. **Click** on **Small Icons**. The smaller icons will be used in the Views Bar.

NOTE

If you hide the Views Bar and later want to display it, open the View menu and click on Views Bar.

Part I Review Questions

1. How do you open FrontPage? *See "Starting FrontPage" in Chapter 1.*

2. What is the purpose of the keyboard shortcuts found on the right side of a menu? *See "Exploring FrontPage" in Chapter 1.*

3. Which view would you select from the Views Bar if you wanted to design a Web page? *See "Understanding the Views Bar" in Chapter 1.*

4. What does WYSIWYG mean? *See "Looking at the Page Layout Views" in Chapter 1.*

5. How many different ways can you get help using FrontPage? *See "Getting Help" in Chapter 1.*

6. How can you add buttons to a toolbar? *See "Changing Toolbar Buttons" in Chapter 2.*

7. Can you remove a button from a toolbar if you find that you never use it? *See "Changing Toolbar Buttons" in Chapter 2.*

8. When you add a new toolbar, where does it appear on the screen? *See "Adding and Removing Toolbars" in Chapter 2.*

9. Is it possible to place more than one toolbar on a line? *See "Moving Toolbars" in Chapter 2.*

10. Where else can you find all the commands shown in the Views Bar? *See "Changing the Look of the Views Bar" in Chapter 2.*

PART II

Creating Your Web Site

3

Designing a Web Site

Now that you've learned your way around the FrontPage screen, it's time to build the basic structure of your Web site. This basic structure consists of a Home Page (the main page of your Web site) and a few pages that are attached (linked) to it. Your Home Page is the introduction and starting place for your Web site. It is the first page that visitors see when they access your site from the Internet. The pages attached to it cover the topics introduced in your Home Page. In this chapter, you'll learn how to:

- Get a quick start building your Web site's foundation
- Select your browser audience
- Use the pre-designed themes that come with FrontPage
- Name your Web pages
- Create borders that have the same content on every page
- Open and close your Web site

Following the Web Wizard

FrontPage contains a number of templates that make it easy for you to start building your Web site. The simplest template is the Personal Web, and it's the one recommended for novice Web designers. The Personal Web creates a Home Page and three linked pages with placeholders for text and graphics.

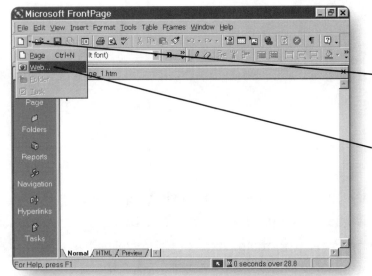

1. **Click** on the **down arrow** to the right of the New Page icon. A menu will appear.

2. **Click** on **Web**. The New dialog box will open.

3. **Click** on the **Personal Web icon**. The Personal Web will be selected.

TIP

If you want to use a Web site or Web page that you've found on the Internet as a template for your Web site, select Import Web Wizard. This wizard will walk you through the steps needed to download the site or page to your computer.

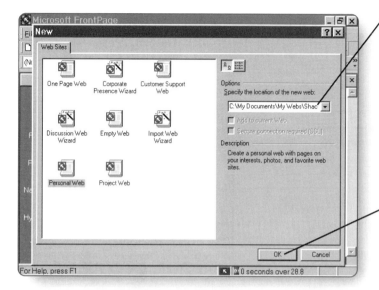

4. **Click** in the **Specify the location of the new web text box** and **type** the **path** to the directory in which you want to store your Web pages. This directory does not need to be one that already exists on your computer. FrontPage will create it for you.

5. **Click** on **OK**. A confirmation dialog box will open.

NOTE

If you want to store your Web in the default directory, add a subdirectory in which to store your work. Just type a backslash and the subdirectory name after the default path.

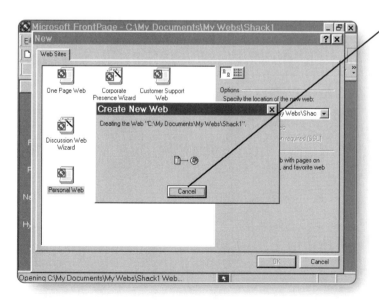

6. **Wait** while FrontPage creates a Web site for you based on the template that you chose. When FrontPage is finished, the Page View screen will return.

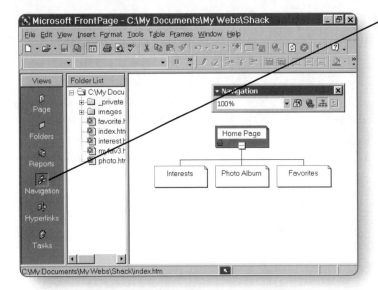

7. Click on the **Navigation view button**. A chart showing how the Web site is arranged will appear in the right side of the window. The Folder List will open to the left of the chart. The Folder List displays all the files and folders that make up the Web site.

Targeting Your Browser Audience

One of your goals as a Web designer is to create a site that can be viewed by the largest number of visitors. This means that your site needs to be compatible with a variety of browsers. By using the FrontPage compatibility feature, you can select the browsers (and version number of the browser) with which you want your site to work best.

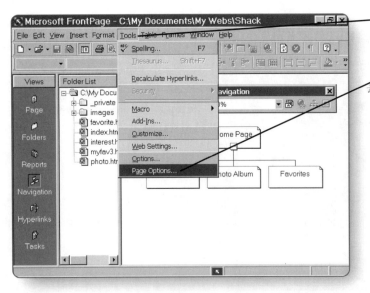

1. Click on **Tools**. The Tools menu will appear.

2. Click on **Page Options**. The Page Options dialog box will open.

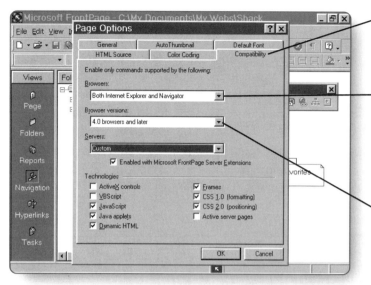

3. Click on the **Compatibility tab**. The Compatibility tab will come forward.

4. Click on the **down arrow** next to the Browsers list box and **click** on **Both Internet Explorer and Navigator**. The option will appear in the list box.

5. Click on the **down arrow** next to the Browser Versions list box and **click** on **4.0 browsers and later**. The option will appear in the list box.

NOTE

As you select options from the list boxes, the options available in the Technologies area will change. If there is an option that you would like to enable, click on it to place a check in the check box.

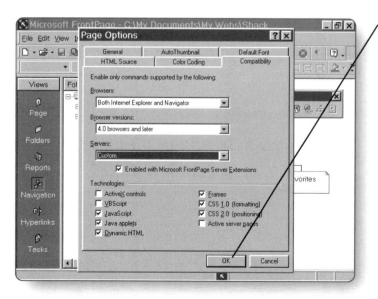

6. Click on **OK**. The compatibility options will be enabled, and FrontPage will only accept the addition of Web page features that are supported by the browsers you select.

Giving Your Web Site a Theme

You don't need to be a graphic designer to make your Web site look good. FrontPage includes a number of themes to help you make your Web site more attractive. Each theme contains color coordinated and graphically pleasing fonts, bullets, banners, and navigation bars. Themes can be applied to an entire Web site or to individual pages. If you want to create your own look, you can make changes to a theme or choose not to use any of the themes that come with FrontPage.

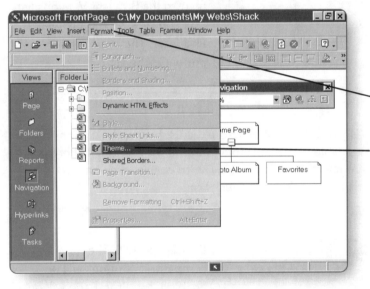

Applying a Theme to Your Entire Web Site

1. **Click** on **Format**. The Format menu will appear.

2. **Click** on **Theme**. The Themes dialog box will open.

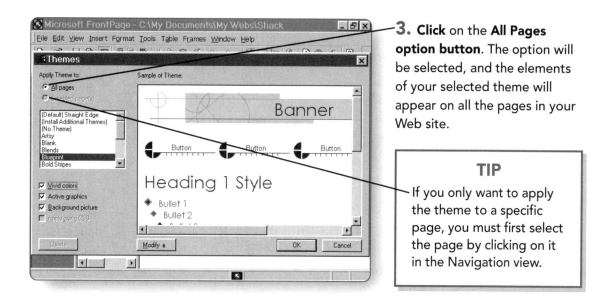

3. Click on the **All Pages option button**. The option will be selected, and the elements of your selected theme will appear on all the pages in your Web site.

TIP

If you only want to apply the theme to a specific page, you must first select the page by clicking on it in the Navigation view.

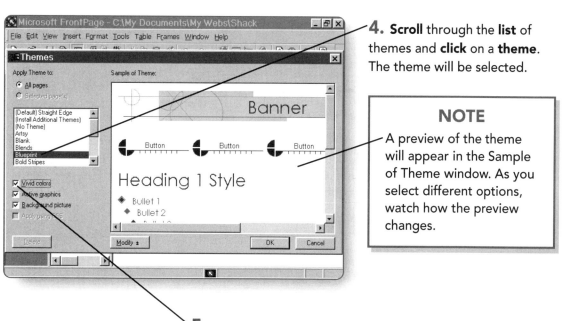

4. Scroll through the **list** of themes and **click** on a **theme**. The theme will be selected.

NOTE

A preview of the theme will appear in the Sample of Theme window. As you select different options, watch how the preview changes.

5. Click on **Vivid Colors** to use brightly colored text and graphics on certain theme components. A check will appear in the box.

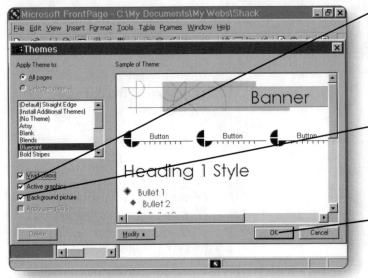

6. Click on **Active Graphics** to animate certain theme components such as navigation buttons and bullets. A check will appear in the box.

7. Click on **Background Picture** to use a patterned background on your Web pages. A check will appear in the box.

8. Click on **OK**. The theme will be applied to all the pages within your Web site.

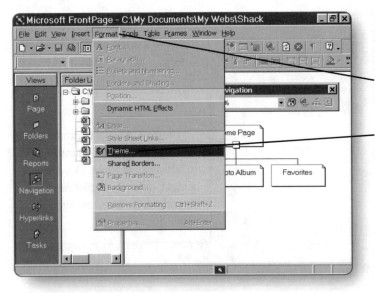

Modifying the Theme

1. Click on **Format**. The Format menu will appear.

2. Click on **Theme**. The Themes dialog box will open.

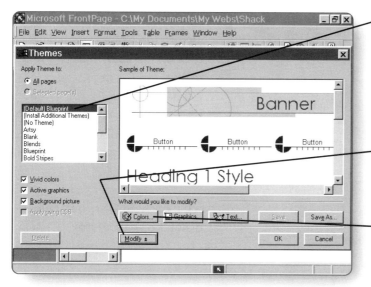

3. Click on the **theme** that you want to use as the basis for your personalized theme. The theme will be selected and a preview will show in the Sample of Theme window.

4. Click on **Modify**. A row of buttons for the theme elements that you can change will appear.

5. Click on **Colors**. The Modify Theme dialog box will appear.

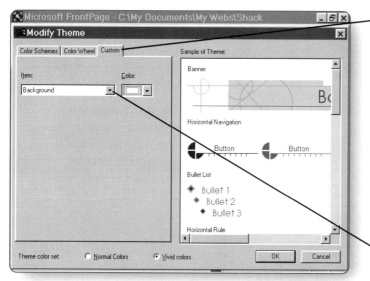

6. Click on the **Custom tab**. The Custom tab will come forward.

NOTE

If you want to use the color scheme from a different theme, click on the Color Schemes tab and select the theme.

7. Click the **down arrow** next to the Item list box. A list of page elements will appear.

8. Click on the **item** to which you want to apply a color change. The item will appear in the list box.

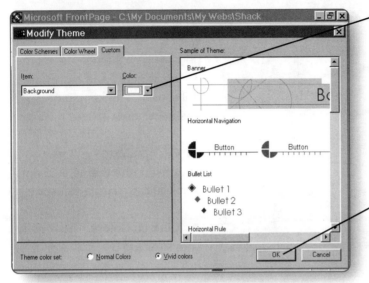

9. **Click** on the **down arrow** next to the Color list box and **click** on the **color** that you want to apply to the item. The color will be selected. As you make changes to the different items, you'll see the effect of each change in the Sample of Theme window.

10. **Click** on **OK**. The Themes dialog box will return.

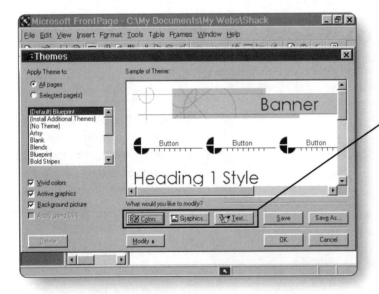

11. **Click** on **OK**. A confirmation dialog box will appear.

TIP

You can change the images for graphic elements, such as bullets and horizontal lines, contained in the theme.

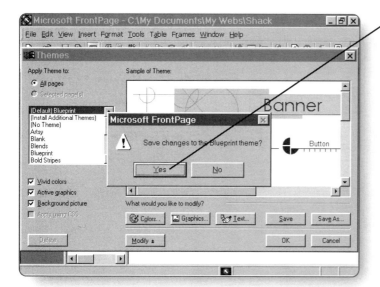

12. Click on **Yes**. The Save Theme dialog box will appear.

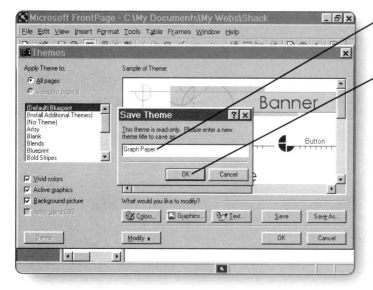

13. Type a different **name** for the theme in the text box.

14. Click on **OK**. Your new theme will be applied to each page in your Web site.

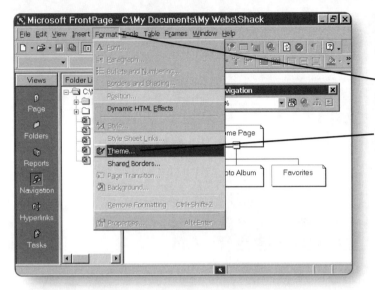

Working without a Theme

1. **Click** on **Format**. The Format menu will appear.

2. **Click** on **Theme**. The Themes dialog box will open.

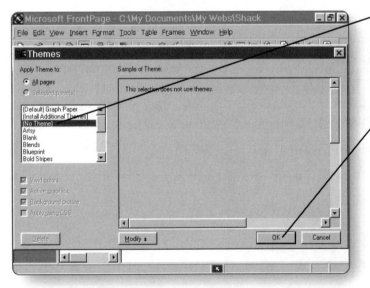

3. **Click** on **(No Theme)** in the list of themes. The No Theme option will be selected and the Sample of Theme window will be blank.

4. **Click** on **OK**. The pages in your Web site will not contain any theme colors, images, or other theme elements.

NOTE

The Web site used as an example in this book does not use a theme.

Renaming Web Pages

The titles that FrontPage assigns to pages in your Web site provide examples of how you might title your own Web pages. You'll want to give each one of your pages a new title that describes its unique content.

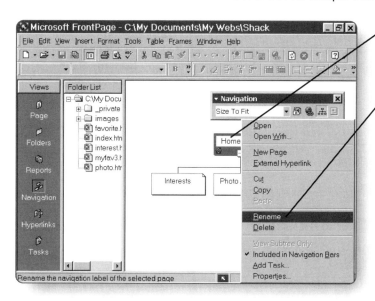

1. **Right-click** on a **page icon** in the Navigation view. A menu will appear.

2. **Click** on **Rename**. The default title will be highlighted within the page icon.

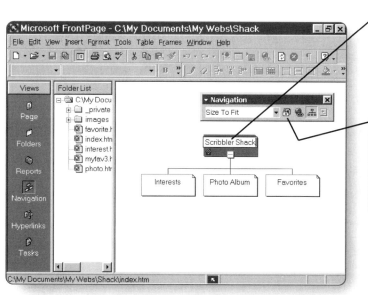

3. **Type** a new **title** for the page.

TIP

Click on the Portrait/ Landscape button on the Navigation toolbar to change the orientation of the organization chart.

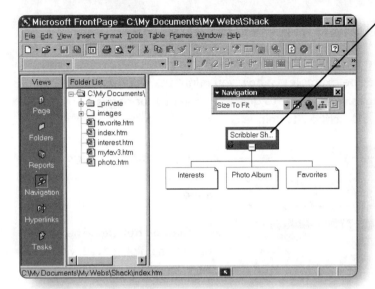

4. Press the **Enter key**. The title of the Web page will change.

TIP

You can also rename files by right-clicking on any file in the Folder List and selecting Rename from the menu that appears.

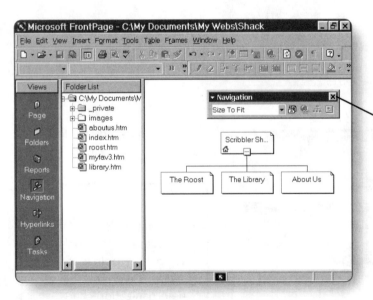

5. Rename the other **pages** in your Web site.

TIP

You can close the Navigation toolbar by clicking on the Close button. To view the toolbar again, click on View on the menu bar, select Toolbars, and then select Navigation.

Setting Shared Border Frames

Shared borders allow you to add text, graphics, or navigation controls to one page in your Web site and then apply the same elements automatically to all remaining pages.

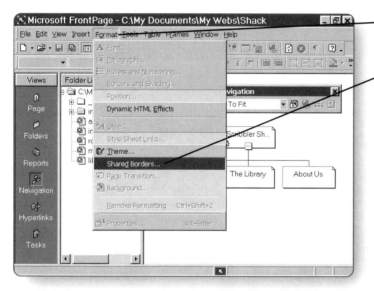

1. Click on **Format**. The Format menu will appear.

2. Click on **Shared Borders**. The Shared Borders dialog box will open.

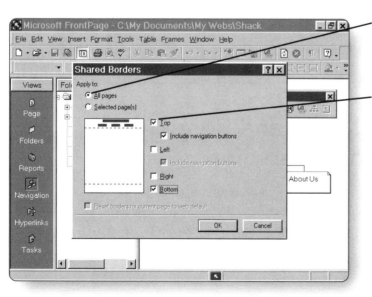

3. Click on the **All Pages option button**. The option will be selected.

4. Click on **Top**, **Left**, **Right**, or **Bottom** to add a frame along the corresponding sides of every page in your Web site. A check mark will appear in each selected box.

NOTE

When working with a theme, you must check the Top frame to view banners that FrontPage automatically applies to each page.

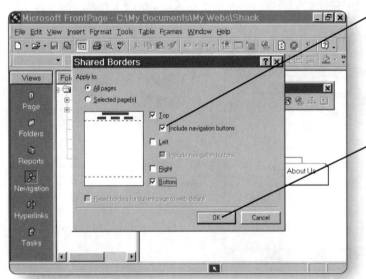

5. **Click** in the **Include navigation buttons check box** to add navigation controls for your Web site to a shared border. A check will appear in the box.

6. **Click** on **OK**. The border frames and navigation controls will be applied to the entire Web site.

NOTE

You'll learn more about navigation controls in Chapter 6, "Working with Hyperlinks."

Closing and Reopening Your Web Site

Before you leave your computer, you may want to close your Web site and FrontPage. When you come back, you'll need to reopen the program and find your Web site.

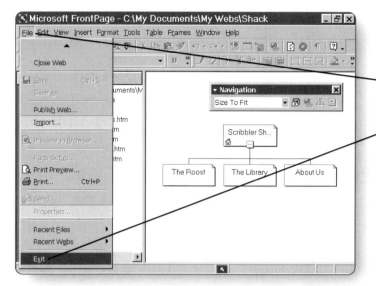

Closing Your Web Site

1. Click on **File**. The File menu will appear.

2. Click on **Exit**. FrontPage will close.

Opening Your Web Site

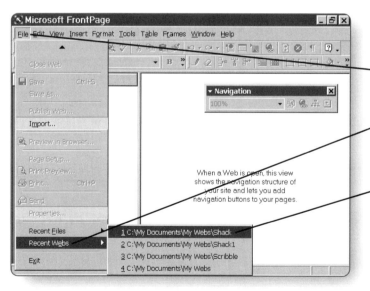

1. Open FrontPage. FrontPage will open on your screen.

2. Click on **File**. The File menu will appear.

3. Click on **Recent Webs**. A second menu will appear.

4. Click on the **Web site** with which you want to work. The Web site will open. If your Web site doesn't appear in this list, there is another option for finding it.

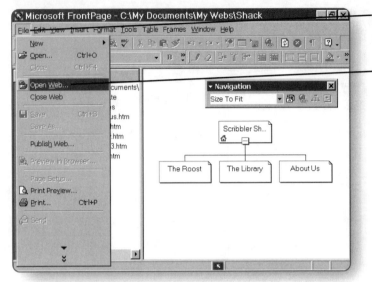

5. **Click** on **File**. The File menu will appear.

6. **Click** on **Open Web**. The Open Web dialog box will appear.

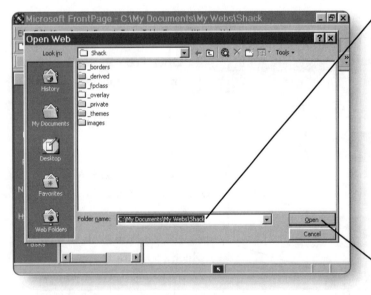

7. In the Folder name text box, **type** the **drive and directory path** for the Web site that you want to open.

NOTE

You can also use the Look in list box to search for the directory where the Web site is located.

8. **Click** on **Open**. The Web site will open.

4

Building Your Web Pages

You've spent enough time getting familiar with FrontPage and planning your Web site. Now it's time to attack the real heart of your Web site—the individual Web pages. You're probably anxious to start adding words and pictures to those pages. In this chapter, you'll learn how to:

- Open Web pages so that you can work with them
- Insert new text and graphics
- Edit your text and graphics
- Add text to shared borders
- Apply different format styles to text
- Undo and redo your work (when you change your mind)
- Save your Web pages

Opening Web Pages for Editing

In the first few chapters, you learned how to start building your Web site. Now that you have a structure on which to hang your Web site, it's time to add some content to each of the pages. But first, you'll need to know how to open individual pages and switch between them. Before you begin, you'll need to open the Web site that you created in Chapter 3.

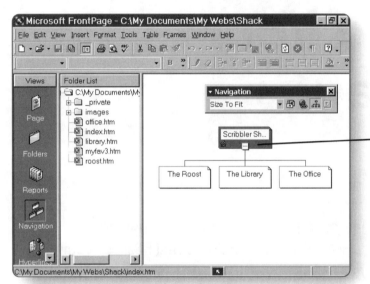

1. Double-click on a **page icon** in the Navigation view. The page will appear in the Page view window.

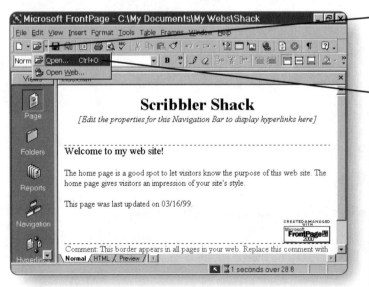

2. Click on the down arrow next to the **Open** button. A menu will appear.

3. Click on **Open**. The Open File dialog box will open.

NOTE

If you enabled the navigation bars when you set up the shared borders, each page of your Web site will include hyperlinks to your other Web pages.

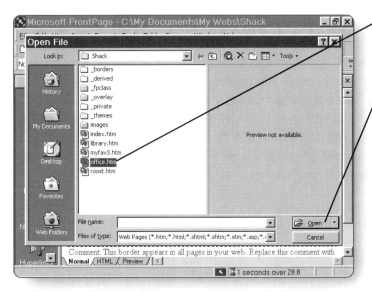

4. **Click** on **another Web page** that you want to open. The file will be selected.

5. **Click** on **Open**. The page will appear in the Page view window. The first Web page that you opened will remain open but will be located behind this second page.

6. **Click** on **Window** on the menu bar. The Window menu will appear. The lower half of this menu will list all of the files that are currently open and the file that is displayed in the program window will be preceded by a check.

7. **Select** the **Web page** that you want to see in the Page view window. The page will be displayed.

Inserting Text and Graphics

Text and graphics make up the largest portion of a Web page. In order to begin the construction process, you'll need to replace the text and images that are used as placeholders with your own work. You'll have to come up with the words on your own, but FrontPage includes a Clip Art collection with thousands of pictures from which to choose. These offer you a great way to give your Web pages color.

Selecting Text

Many text-editing commands require that you first select the text. This section will show you how to select text using several methods.

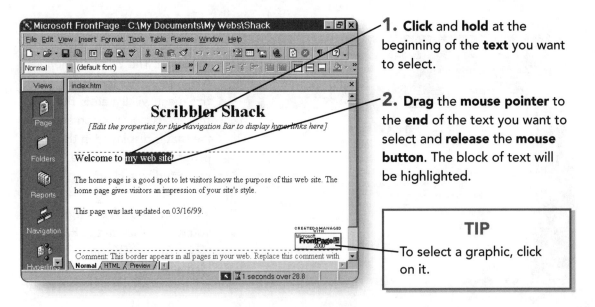

1. **Click** and **hold** at the beginning of the **text** you want to select.

2. **Drag** the **mouse pointer** to the **end** of the text you want to select and **release** the **mouse button**. The block of text will be highlighted.

TIP

To select a graphic, click on it.

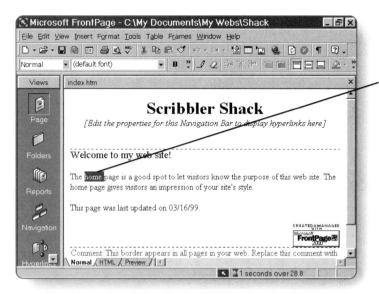

3. Select text using one of the following shortcuts:

- Select one word by clicking twice on the word.

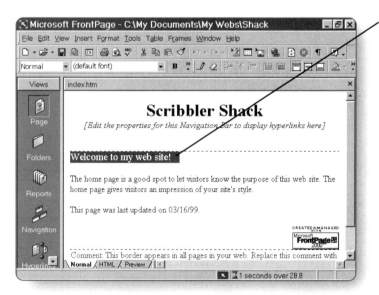

- Select a line by placing the mouse pointer on the left margin (the pointer will change to an arrow) and clicking once next to the line.

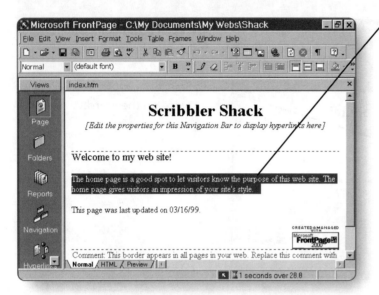

Select several lines by placing the mouse pointer on the left margin. Then press and hold the mouse button while you drag the mouse pointer next to each line that you want to select.

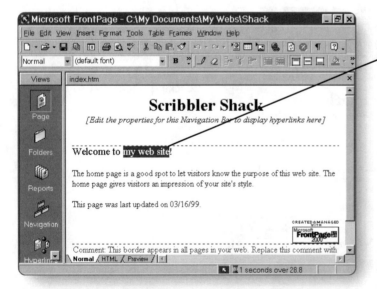

Adding Text

1. Select the **text** that you want to replace with your own words.

NOTE

The new text that you type will use the same paragraph and character formatting as the replaced text.

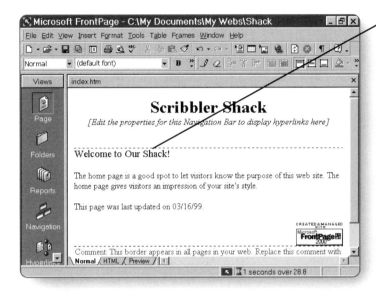

2. Type your new **text**. The new text will replace the text you selected.

3. Click in the **position** where you want to add text. The insertion bar will appear on the page in the selected position.

NOTE

You may want start your Home Page with a few sentences or paragraphs that describe what your visitors will find in your Web site. Or, you may want to tell a story, talk about your profession, or share your hobbies.

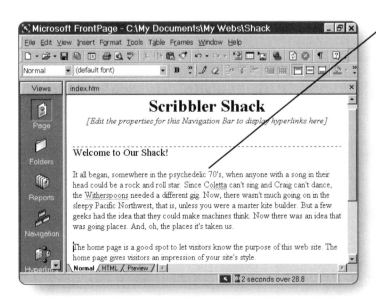

4. Type some **text**.

5. Press the **Enter key** at the end of each paragraph. The next paragraph will start on a new line.

Adding Clip Art

1. Click on the **place** where you want to insert an image. The insertion bar will appear.

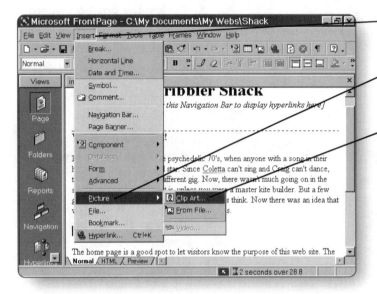

2. Click on **Insert**. The Insert menu will appear.

3. Click on **Picture**. A second menu will appear.

4. Click on **Clip Art**. The Clip Art Gallery dialog box will open with the Pictures tab displayed.

TIP

If you want to add special characters (such as copyright or trademark symbols) to your Web page, select Symbol from the Insert menu.

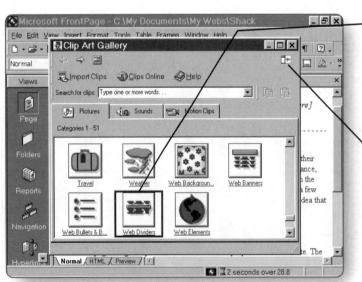

5. Click on the **category** of clip art for which you are looking. The clip art in that category will appear in the preview pane.

TIP

Click on the Change to Small Window button to display a narrower window.

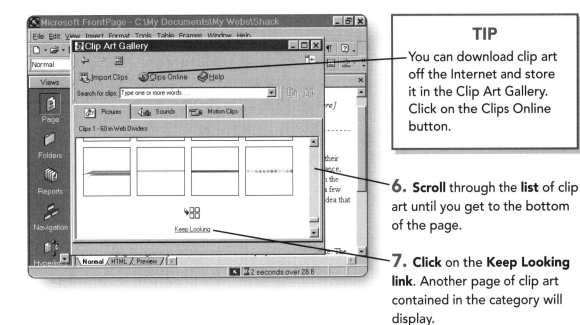

TIP

You can download clip art off the Internet and store it in the Clip Art Gallery. Click on the Clips Online button.

6. Scroll through the **list** of clip art until you get to the bottom of the page.

7. Click on the **Keep Looking link**. Another page of clip art contained in the category will display.

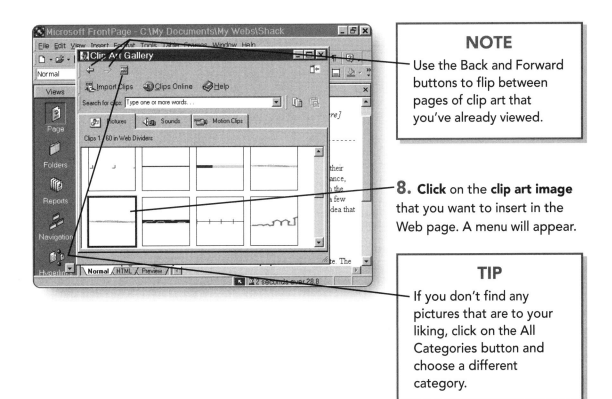

NOTE

Use the Back and Forward buttons to flip between pages of clip art that you've already viewed.

8. Click on the **clip art image** that you want to insert in the Web page. A menu will appear.

TIP

If you don't find any pictures that are to your liking, click on the All Categories button and choose a different category.

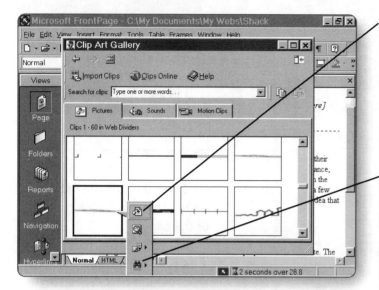

9. Click on the **Insert Clip button.** The picture will be added to your Web page at the selected position and the Clip Art Gallery will close.

TIP

If you find a picture that is almost, but not quite what you were looking for, click on the Find Similar Clips button. The Clip Art Gallery can help you search for that perfect picture.

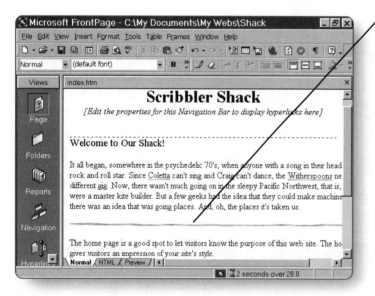

The clip art will appear on the Web page in the selected location.

NOTE

You'll learn how to position images next to text to create an appealing look in Chapter 9, "Working With Graphics."

Editing Your Text and Graphics

You've got a great start on your Web page, but you may still need to do some editing. If you've placed something on a page and later decide that you don't want to use it, you can always delete it. You can move text and images to different locations on a page, or you can make a copy to put in another location.

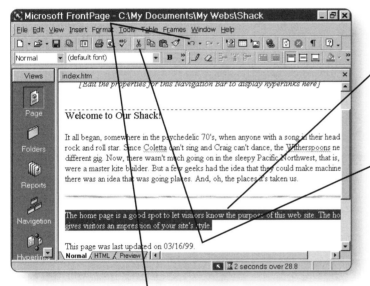

Deleting Text and Graphics

1. Select the **text or graphic** that you want to delete. The text or graphic will be highlighted.

2. Click on the **Cut button** (you can also press the Delete key on the keyboard). The text or graphic will be deleted.

TIP

You can delete text and graphics immediately after you have placed them on a page by clicking the Undo button.

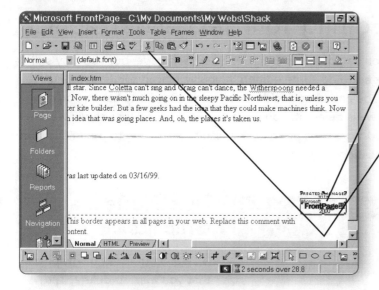

Moving Text and Graphics

1. **Select** the **text** or **graphic** to be moved. The text or graphic will be highlighted.

2. **Click** on the **Cut button**. The text or graphic will disappear from the page and will be stored in the Windows clipboard.

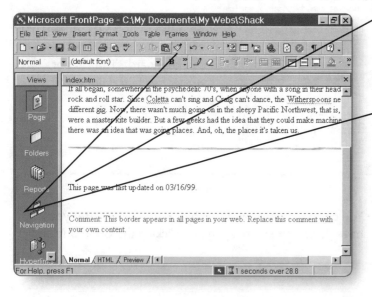

3. **Click** on the **place** where you want the text or graphic moved. The insertion bar will appear.

4. **Click** on the **Paste button**. The text or graphic will appear in the new position.

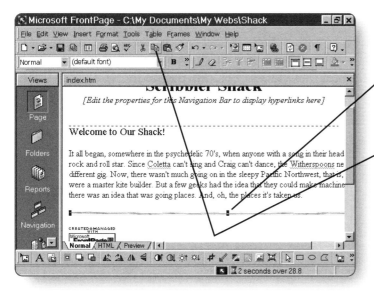

Copying Text and Graphics

1. Select the **text or graphic** to be copied. The text or graphic will be highlighted.

2. Click on the **Copy button**. A copy of the text or graphic will be stored in the Windows clipboard.

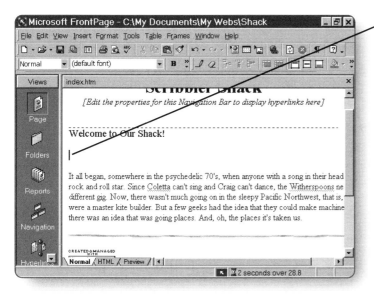

3. Click on the **place** where you want to put a copy of the text or graphic. The insertion bar will appear.

4. Click on the **Paste button**. The text or graphic will be copied to the new position.

Adding Text to Shared Borders

If you are using the shared borders feature, you'll see the borders at the sides of your Web pages. These shared borders are separated from the main part of the Web page by a dotted line.

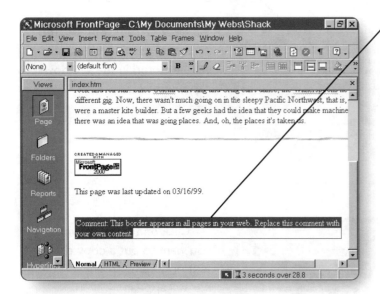

1. Click on the **text** inside the shared border. The text will be highlighted and the shared border will appear as a solid line.

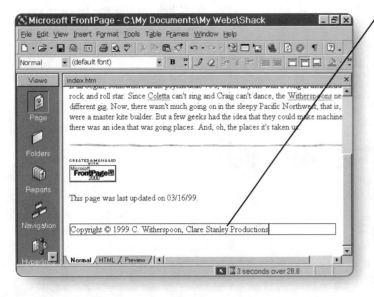

2. Type the **text** that you want to see within that border (which will appear on every page in your Web site).

TIP

The bottom border is a good place to put copyright information to protect your page, or to give your e-mail address so that visitors to your site can send you a message.

Using Format Styles

FrontPage uses HTML styles that can be interpreted by any Web browser to display formatted text. It is a good idea to use paragraph styles to format your text.

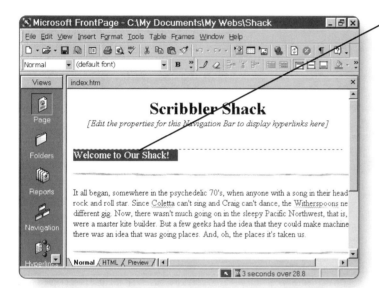

1. Select the **paragraph** that you want to format.

NOTE

Use the Font Size list box to change the size of selected text.

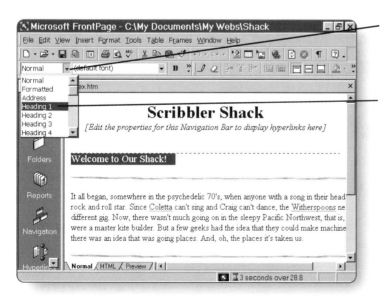

2. Click on the **down arrow** in the Style field. A drop-down list of style options will appear.

3. Click on a **style** that you want to use. The paragraph will appear in the style that you chose.

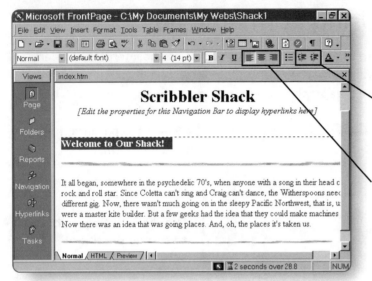

4. Click on one or more **Formatting toolbar buttons** to change the appearance of the text to fit your needs:

- To change the indent of a paragraph, click on the Increase Indent or Decrease Indent button.

- To change the paragraph alignment, select the paragraph and click on the Align Left, Center, or Align Right button.

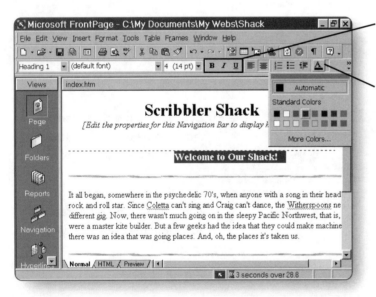

- To emphasize text, select the text and click on the Bold, Italic, or Underline button.

- To change the text color, click on the Font Color button.

Undoing and Redoing Your Work

As you are working on a page, you'll be making lots of changes. There will be times when you make a change and then decide that you don't like the result. Or maybe you'll make a mistake and want to undo that mistake. Here's how to undo and redo both a single action and a series of actions.

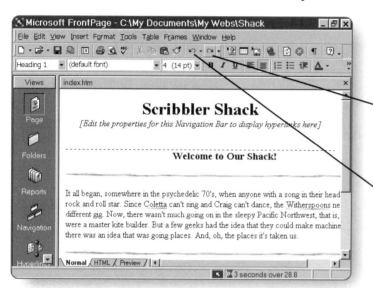

- Click on the Redo button to reverse the effect of the last undo command that you performed.

- Click on the Undo button to reverse the last action you performed.

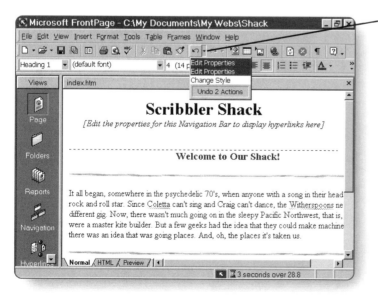

- Click on the down arrow next to the Undo or Redo button to display the list of the last 30 actions you performed. Move the mouse pointer down the list and click on the last action that you want to reverse.

Saving Your Web Pages

The importance of saving your work can't be stressed enough. Computers are subject to a number of factors that can cause them to crash. Crashes may be caused by something as simple as an electrical surge or outage, or by something more complex, such as a hardware problem. To protect yourself from lost work, save your Web pages every few minutes.

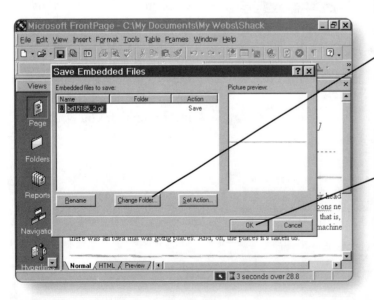

1. **Click** on the **Save button**. If you've added images to the Web page, the Save Embedded Files dialog box will open.

NOTE

If you've only added text to the page, the file will immediately be saved when you click on the Save button. You don't need to do anything else.

---

2. **Click** on the **Change Folder button**. The Change Folder dialog box will open.

NOTE

If you want to save the graphic in the default folder location, click on OK.

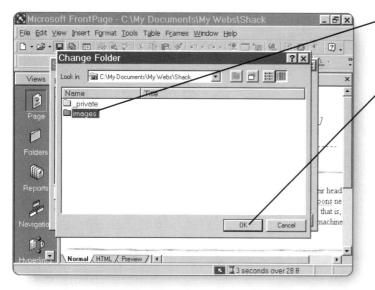

3. **Click** on the **folder** in which you want to save the graphic. The folder will be selected.

4. **Click** on **OK**. The Save Embedded Files dialog box will appear.

TIP

You can create a new folder in which to store files by clicking on the Create New Folder button.

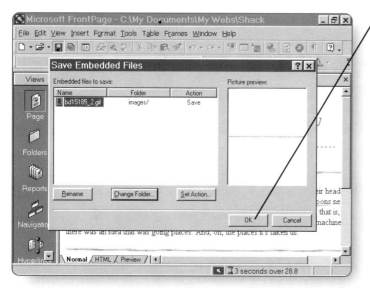

5. **Click** on **OK**. The Web page will be saved.

5

Managing and Printing Your Web Site

As you work with the existing pages in your Web site, you may want to cover more territory, which means adding more pages. Perhaps you want to delete pages that you no longer need. After all this adding and deleting, you may find that some pages need to be moved around. Once you've organized your Web site, you'll need to make sure that you've spelled everything correctly and that it all looks good when viewed in a Web browser. In this chapter, you'll learn how to:

- Create new pages for your Web site
- Reorganize the pages of your Web site
- Check your spelling and correct any spelling mistakes
- Preview Web pages before you publish them on the Internet
- Print hard copies of your Web pages and the Navigation chart

Creating New Pages

The easiest way to add new pages to your Web site is to begin from the Navigation view. By using the Navigation view, you can automatically link new pages to other pages in your Web site. This view also allows you to take advantage of navigation controls that may be contained in your Web site's shared borders. The negative aspect of this method is that newly created pages do not contain any content. If you're looking for a ready-made page, follow the steps for using new page templates in the Page view. Before you begin, you'll need to open the Web site you created in Chapter 3.

Adding a Page in the Navigation View

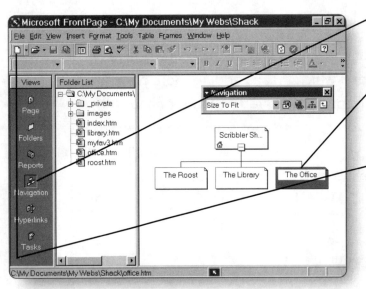

1. Click on the **Navigation view button**. The Navigation view will appear.

2. Click on the **page** to which you want to link the new page. The page will be selected.

3. Click on the **New Page button**. A new blank page will be added to your Web site and will be linked to the page you selected.

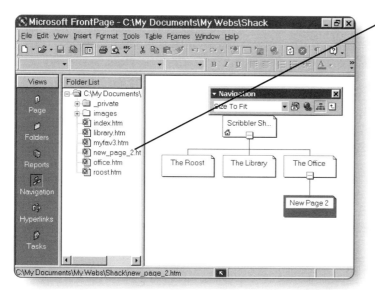

The page that you just added will appear in the Folder List.

TIP

Rename a file by right-clicking on the file in the Folder List and selecting Rename from the menu that appears.

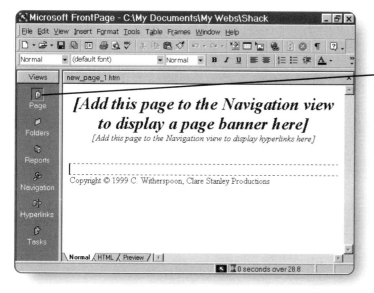

Using a New Page Template

1. Click on the **Page View button**. The Page view will appear.

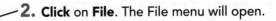

2. **Click** on **File**. The File menu will open.

3. **Click** on **New**. A second menu will appear.

4. **Click** on **Page**. The New dialog box will appear.

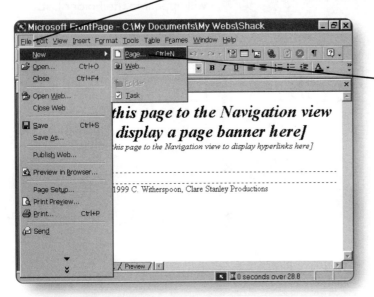

5. **Click** on the **type** of **page** you would like to add to your Web site. The page template will be selected.

6. **Click** on **OK**. The new page will appear in the Page view window.

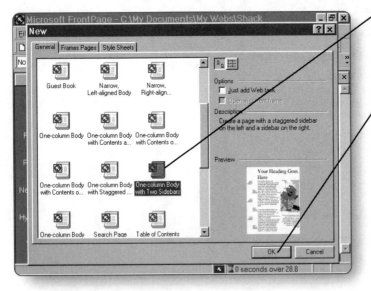

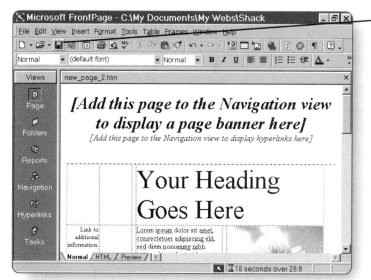

7. Click on the **Save button**. The Save As dialog box will appear.

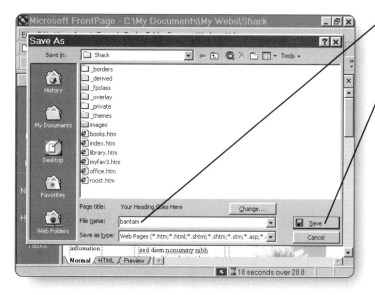

8. Click in the **File name text box** and **type** a different **name** for the file.

9. Click on **Save**. The Web page will be saved.

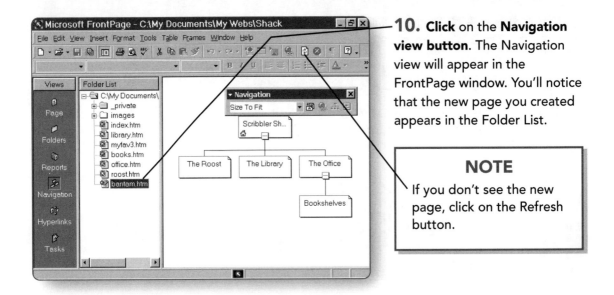

10. Click on the **Navigation view button**. The Navigation view will appear in the FrontPage window. You'll notice that the new page you created appears in the Folder List.

NOTE

If you don't see the new page, click on the Refresh button.

Reorganizing Web Pages

As you are building or updating your Web site, you may find pages that need to be moved or that you no longer need. Pages can be moved easily, and any hyperlinks will be automatically updated. You can also delete pages so that they are removed from your Web site but are still available to you for future use.

Moving Pages Using Drag-and-Drop

When you want to change the structure of your Web site, follow these easy steps to move pages around or to attach a file from the Folder List to the Navigation chart.

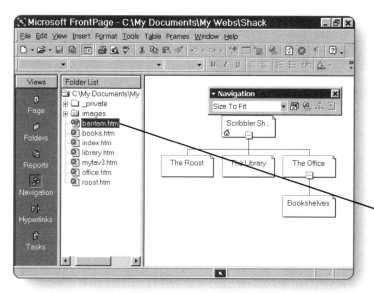

NOTE

When moving or attaching files, you can select a file from the Folder List or choose a page icon in the Navigation chart.

1. Click and hold the **mouse button** on the page that you want to add to or move within the Navigation chart. The page will be selected.

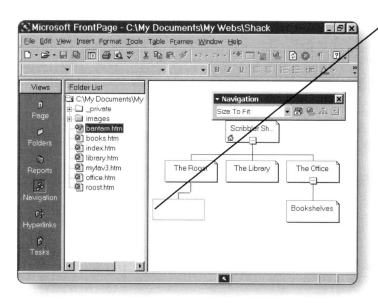

2. Drag the **page** so that it connects to the page with which you want it linked. The moving page will change to an outline. A connecting gray line will show the intended link between it and another page within the Navigation chart.

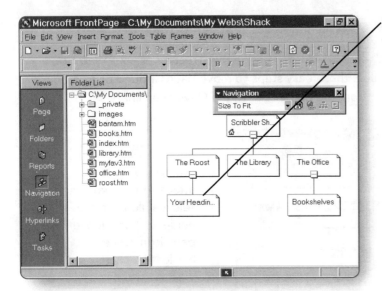

3. Release the **mouse button**. The page will be moved.

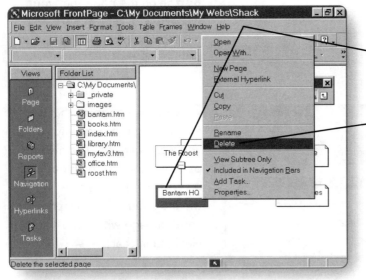

Deleting a Page

1. Right-click on the **page** that you want to remove from your Web site. A menu will appear.

2. Click on **Delete**. The Delete Page dialog box will open.

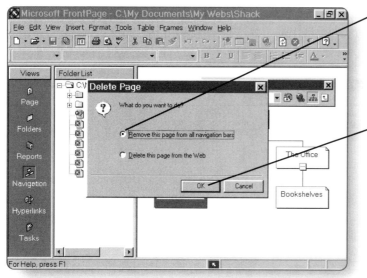

3. **Click** on the **Remove this page from all navigation bars option button**, if it is not already selected. The option will be selected.

4. **Click** on **OK**. The page will be deleted from the Navigation chart but will still be listed in the Folder List. You'll need to move this file to a private folder if you don't want this Web page published on the Internet.

TIP
If you want to completely remove the page from your computer, select the Delete this page from the Web option button.

Using the Private Folder

You could leave pages that you've deleted from the Navigation chart where they are in the Folder List. However, if you do this, you may accidentally publish these pages to your Web site where inquisitive Web surfers may find them. To keep a deleted page for future use and to make it unavailable to visitors, place the page in a private folder.

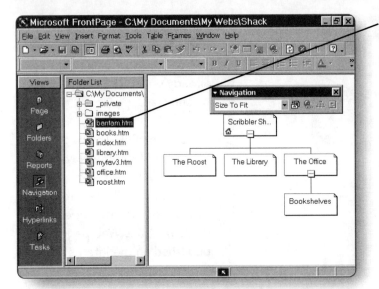

1. Press and hold the **mouse button** on the file in the Folder List. The file will be selected.

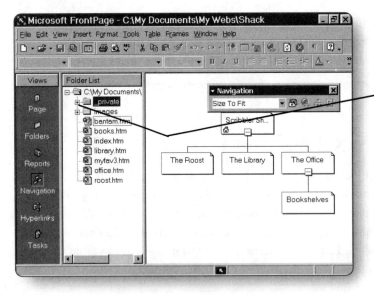

2. Drag the **file** to the _private folder and **release** the **mouse button**. The file will be moved.

3. Click on the **plus sign** next to the _private folder to see the files stored within that folder.

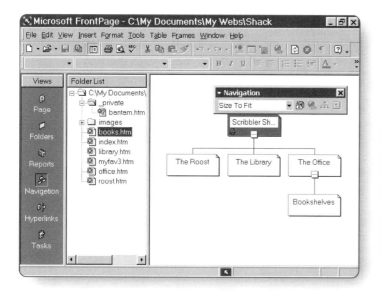

The files in the _private folder will be available for you to use but will not be accessible to anyone visiting your Web site.

NOTE

You can move the page from the _private folder to any place in your Navigation chart by using the drag-and-drop method.

Checking Your Spelling

Before you publish your Web site on the Internet, you'll want to make sure that you've spelled every word correctly. Spelling errors can make even the best Web site look bad.

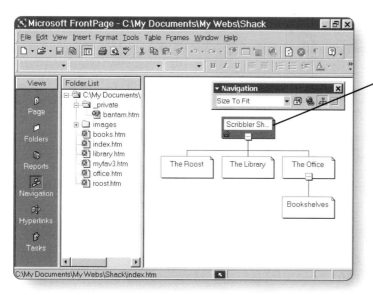

Checking an Individual Page

1. In the Navigation view, **double-click** on the **page** that you want to spell check. The page will open in the Page view.

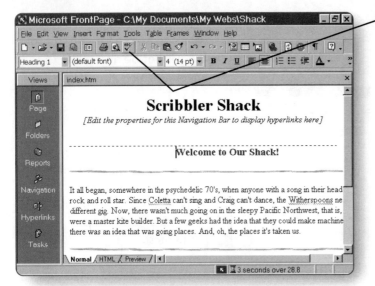

2. Click on the **Check Spelling button.** The Spelling dialog box will open with the first misspelled word displayed in the Not in Dictionary text box.

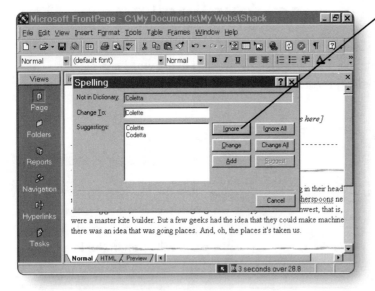

3. Click on the **Ignore button.** The word will be left as is, and the next misspelled word will appear in the Not in Dictionary text box.

TIP

The misspelled word will also be highlighted on the Web page. This will help you determine how to correct the error. To see more of the Web page, click and drag the title bar of the Spelling dialog box to a different location.

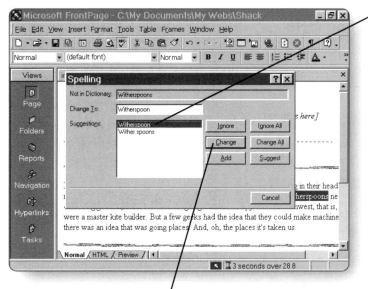

4. **Click** on the **correct spelling** in the Suggestions text box if it is not already listed in the Change To text box. The word will be selected and will appear in the Change To text box.

NOTE

If the correct spelling does not appear in the list, click in the Change To text box and type the word you want.

5. **Click** on the **Change button**. The misspelled word will be replaced by the word selected in the Change To text box and the spell checker will finish checking the page. When the spell check is complete, a confirmation dialog box will appear.

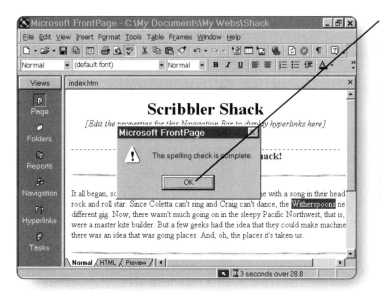

6. **Click** on **OK**. The spell check will be completed.

NOTE

Remember to save your Web pages often so that you don't lose all your hard work.

Checking the Entire Web Site

After you get comfortable working with FrontPage, you'll begin working with multiple pages at one time. When you get to this point, you won't want to spell check each individual page because of the amount of time it would take. It is possible to do one spell check on your entire Web site.

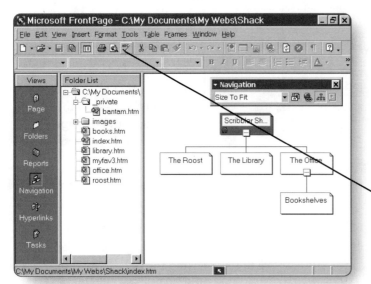

1. Click on the **Navigation view button**. The Navigation view of your Web site will appear.

2. Click on the **Spelling button**. The Spelling dialog box will open.

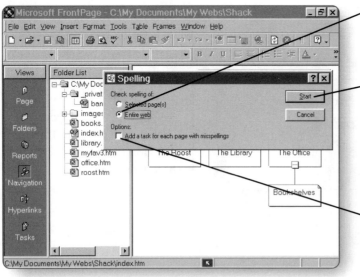

3. Click on the **Entire web option button**. The option will be selected.

4. Click on **Start**. The dialog box will expand showing the status of the spell check and the pages that contain misspelled words.

> ### NOTE
>
> You'll learn about creating tasks and reminders to help you to get your work done in Chapter 14, "Updating Your Web Site."

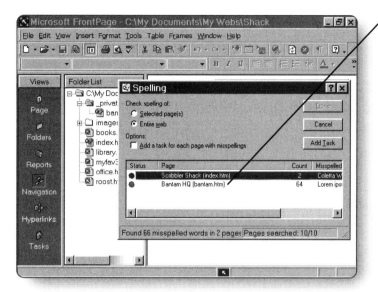

5. Double-click on the **page** that contains the misspelling you want to correct. Another Spelling dialog box will appear with the first misspelled word displayed in the Not in Dictionary text box.

TIP

When you finish correcting the first page, double-click on the next page in the list.

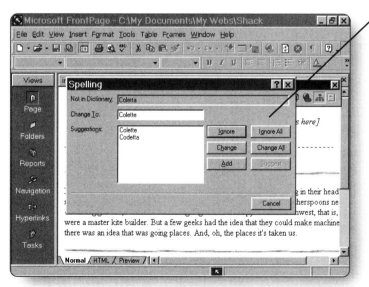

6. Make the appropriate **corrections**. When you have finished with the corrections, the Finished checking documents dialog box will appear.

NOTE

For help using the spell checker, see the previous section, "Checking an Individual Page."

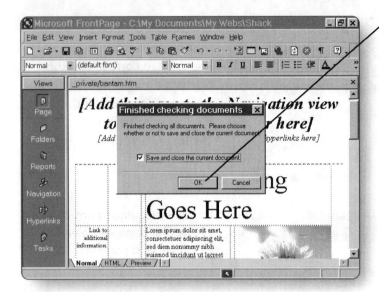

7. Click on **OK**. The Spelling dialog box will return, and the Web page status will be listed as Edited.

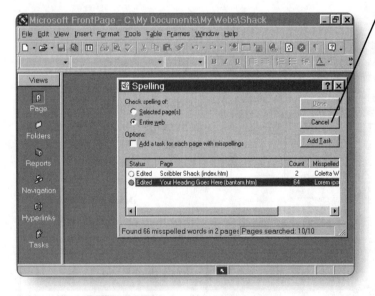

8. Click on **Cancel**. The spell check will be complete.

Previewing Your Web Site

Before you publish your Web pages, you'll want to make sure that you are satisfied with the way they look in a Web browser. If you have Internet Explorer installed on your computer, you can easily preview any Web page from the Preview window.

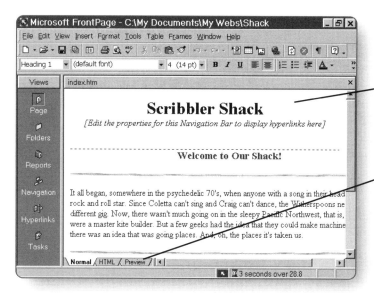

Previewing from FrontPage

1. Open the **Web page** that you want to preview. The page will be displayed in the Page view window.

2. Click on the **Preview tab**. The Web page will appear in the Preview window as it would in the version of Internet Explorer that you have on your computer.

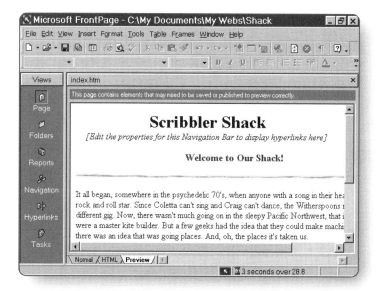

TIP

To view any of the other pages that you created that are linked to this page, press the Ctrl key on your keyboard while you click on a hyperlink.

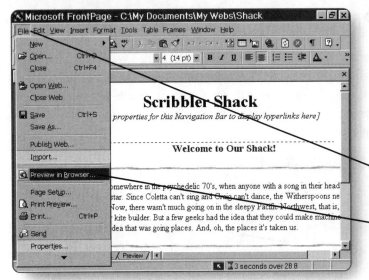

Previewing from a Web Browser

1. Open the **Web page** that you want to preview. The page will be displayed in the Page view window.

2. Click on **File**. The File menu will open.

3. Click on **Preview in Browser**. The Preview in Browser dialog box will appear with a list of the Web browsers that you have installed on your computer.

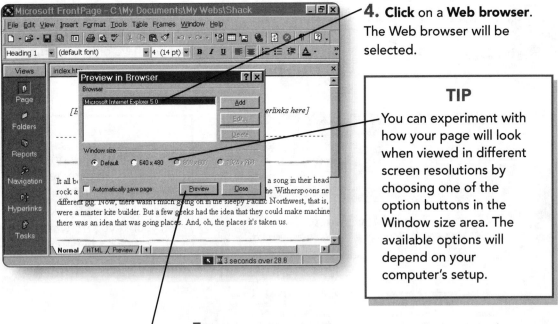

4. Click on a **Web browser**. The Web browser will be selected.

TIP

You can experiment with how your page will look when viewed in different screen resolutions by choosing one of the option buttons in the Window size area. The available options will depend on your computer's setup.

5. Click on **Preview**. The Web page will appear in the selected Web browser.

6. Click on **hyperlinks** to move from page to page within your Web site.

7. Click on the **Close button** of the browser window when you are finished previewing your Web site. The Web browser will close, and you'll return to the Page view of your Web page.

Printing Your Web Site

You may want to print copies of your Web pages. You may also want to print a chart that shows how your Web site is organized. This section will show you how easy printing can be.

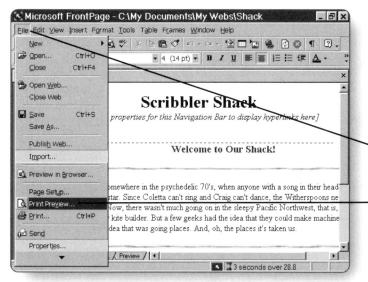

Printing Web Pages

1. Open the **Web page** that you want to print. The Web page will appear in the Page view window.

2. Click on **File**. The File menu will appear.

3. Click on **Print Preview**. The Preview window will appear showing how the page will look when printed.

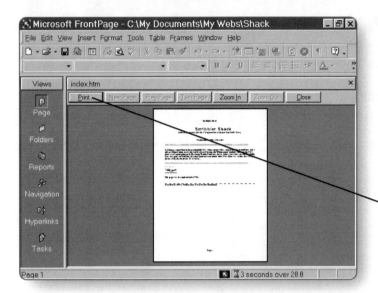

TIP

Use the Zoom In button to see a more detailed preview of the Web page. Use the Zoom Out button to see all of the Web page on the screen.

4. Click on **Print**. The Print dialog box will open.

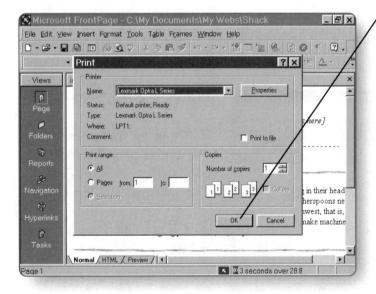

5. Click on **OK**. The page will be sent to your default printer.

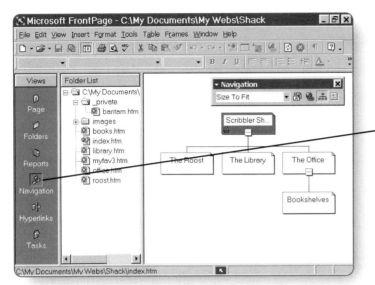

Printing a Site Map

You may want to print a Navigation chart of your Web site.

1. Click on the **Navigation view button**. The Navigation view will appear.

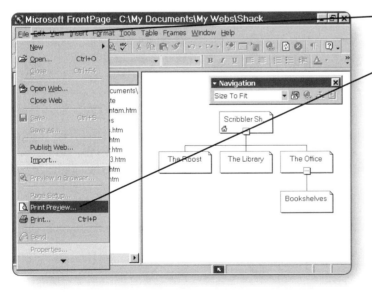

2. Click on **File**. The File menu will appear.

3. Click on **Print Preview**. The Preview window will open.

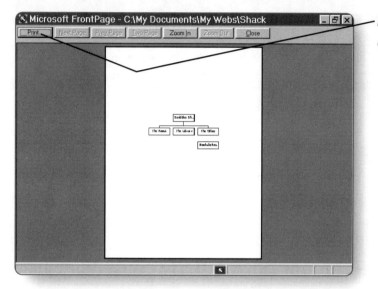

4. Click on **Print**. The Print dialog box will open.

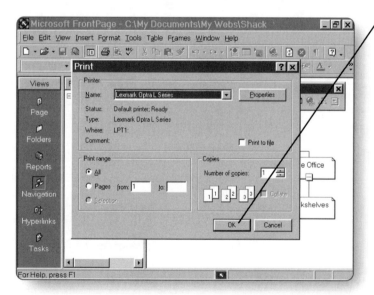

5. Click on **OK**. A Navigation chart of your Web site will print on your default printer.

NOTE

To change to another printer, click on the down arrow next to the Name list box and select the printer from the list.

Part II Review Questions

1. What is the easiest way to get started building a Web site? *See "Following the Web Wizard" in Chapter 3.*

2. Will FrontPage help you create a Web site that is compatible with certain Web browsers? *See "Targeting Your Browser Audience" in Chapter 3.*

3. How can you add images and coordinated colors to your Web site without having to find or create them on your own? *See "Giving Your Web Site a Theme" in Chapter 3.*

4. Is it possible to make changes to the themes that are part of FrontPage? *See "Modifying the Theme" in Chapter 3.*

5. How do you display a Web page so that you can begin adding text, images, and other content to it? *See "Opening Web Pages for Editing" in Chapter 4.*

6. Which toolbar buttons allow you to reposition text and graphics on a Web page? *See "Editing Your Text and Graphics" in Chapter 4.*

7. How can you easily undo an action you've performed while editing a Web page? *See "Undoing and Redoing Your Work" in Chapter 4.*

8. Where can you find page templates that you can use to make creating new pages easier? *See "Creating New Pages" in Chapter 5.*

9. How does using the spell checker on an individual Web page differ from using the spell checker on the entire Web site? *See "Checking Your Spelling" in Chapter 5.*

10. What is the easiest way to view your Web site in a Web browser before you publish it to the Internet? *See "Previewing Your Web Site" in Chapter 5.*

PART III

Expanding Your Web Site

6

Working with Hyperlinks

Hyperlinks can take your visitors to any page of your site that you want them to see. Hyperlinks let you share some of your favorite places on the Internet or direct visitors to places where they can find more information about a subject discussed in your Web site. If you want to give visitors an easy way to correspond with you, you can create a hyperlink that will address an e-mail message to you. In this chapter, you'll learn how to:

- Direct visitors to pages and bookmarks within your Web site
- Create links to share other interesting Web sites with visitors
- Give your visitors an easy way to send you an e-mail message
- Make changes to hyperlinks that you've created
- Select hyperlink colors to help visitors track their path through your site
- Set navigation controls to help visitors navigate through your Web site

Creating Links Inside Your Web Site

Navigation bars (which you learned about in Chapter 3) provide one way to move around a Web site. You can also use hyperlinks to browse from page to page within a site. These hyperlinks can point visitors to a specific page or to a specific place on a page. Hyperlinks can also open a word processing or slide show file in a visitor's Web browser. If you can put it in your Web site, you can create a link that points to it.

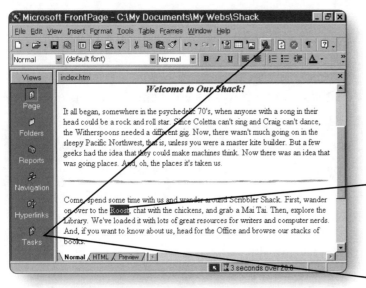

Linking to an Existing Page

1. Open the **page** that will contain the hyperlink to an existing page within your Web site. The open page will appear in the Page view window.

2. Select the **text or graphic** that you want to use as the link. The text or graphic will be highlighted.

3. Click on the **Hyperlink button**. The Create Hyperlink dialog box will open.

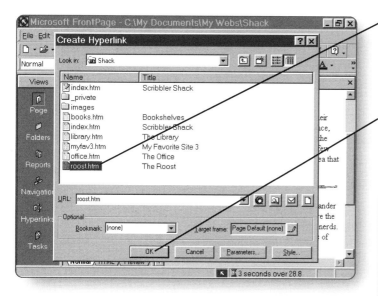

4. Click on the **page** to which the open page will link. The file name will appear in the URL text box.

5. Click on **OK**. The hyperlink will be created.

TIP

Image hyperlinks are surrounded by an outline. To remove the line, right-click on the image and select Image Properties. Click on the Appearance tab and set the Border Thickness to 0.

Creating a Link to a New Page

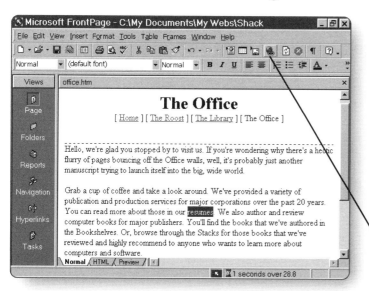

1. Open the **page** that will contain the hyperlink to a new Web page. The open page will appear in the Page view window.

2. Select the **text** or **graphic** that you want to use as the link. The text or graphic will be highlighted.

3. Click on the **Hyperlink button**. The Create Hyperlink dialog box will open.

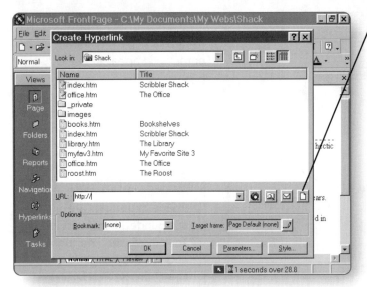

4. Click on the **Create a Page and Link to the New Page button**. The New dialog box will open.

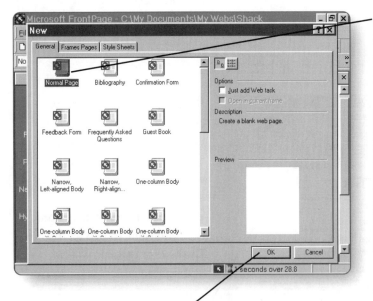

5. Click on the **template** page that you want to use for the new page. The template will be displayed in the Preview pane.

NOTE

Look at the Description and Preview sections of the New dialog for more information about the selected template.

6. Click on **OK**. The new page will appear in the Page view window.

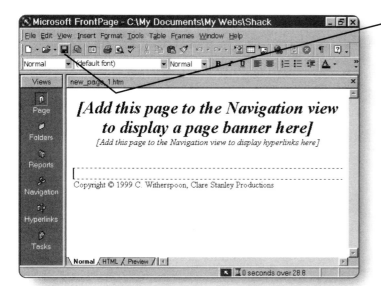

7. **Click** on the **Save button**. The Save As dialog box will appear.

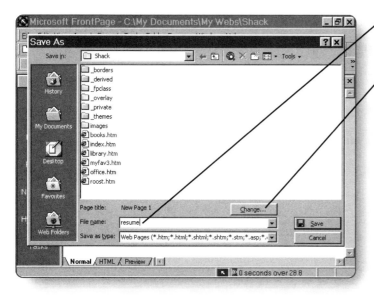

8. **Type** a **file name** for the new page in the File name text box.

9. **Click** on the **Change button**. The Set Page Title dialog box will open and let you give your new page a descriptive name.

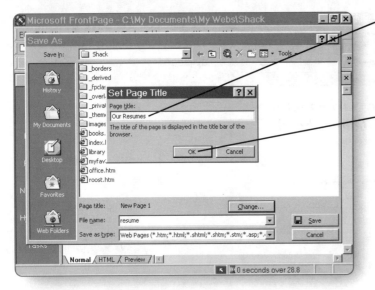

10. **Click** in the **Page title text box** and **type** a **title** for the page, if you want to change the default title of the Web page.

11. **Click** on **OK**. The Save As dialog box will appear.

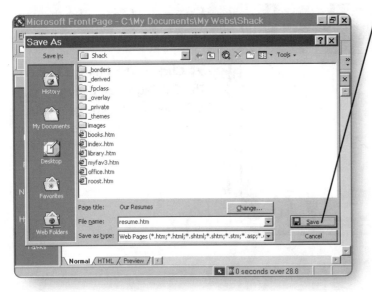

12. **Click** on **Save**. The Web page will be saved with the new file name and title.

TIP

You can delete and rename files from the Save As dialog box. Click on the file that you want to change and select the appropriate command from the Tools drop-down list.

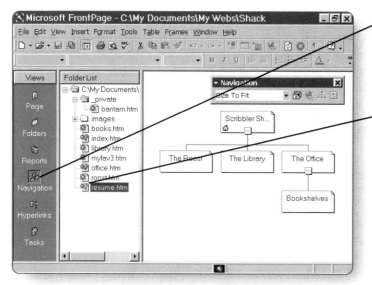

13. **Click** on the **Navigation view button**. The Navigation chart of your Web site will appear in the view window.

14. In the Folder list, **click and hold** the **mouse button** on the file that you just created. The page will be selected.

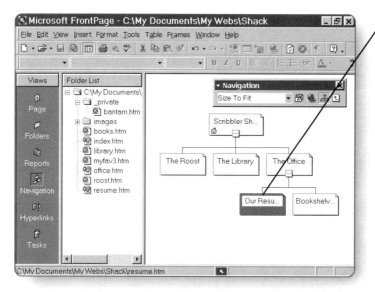

15. **Drag** the **page** so that it connects to the page from which you created the hyperlink (the page you opened in step 1). The new page will turn into an outline.

16. **Release** the **mouse button**. The page will be added to your site's Navigation chart.

Creating Links to Bookmarks

Bookmarks are hyperlinks that will take your visitors to a specific place on a specific page within your Web site. Bookmarks work well if you have a large amount of information on a page and you don't want to make your visitors wade through all of it. Creating this type of hyperlink involves a two step process. First, determine where you want to place a bookmark; then create the hyperlink that will send your visitors to the bookmarked location within your site.

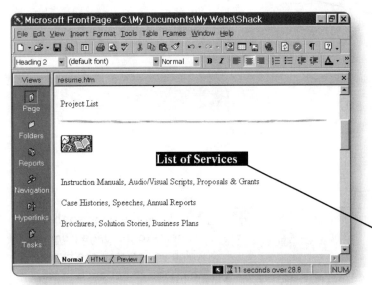

1. Open the **page** that will contain the bookmark. The page will appear in the Page view window.

2. Select the **text or graphic** that you want to use as the bookmark. The text or graphic will be highlighted.

3. Click on **Insert**. The Insert menu will appear.

4. Click on **Bookmark**. The Bookmark dialog box will open.

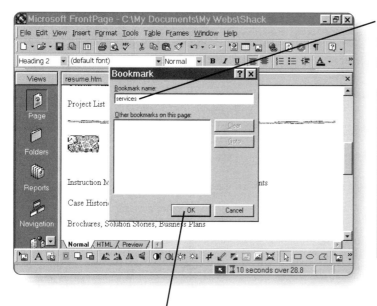

5. **Click** in the **Bookmark Name text box** and **type** a **name** for the bookmark.

NOTE

It is usually best to use the old DOS 8.3 rule when naming pages, files, and bookmarks in your Web site. Your file names should be no longer than 8 characters.

6. **Click** on **OK**. The bookmark will be created.

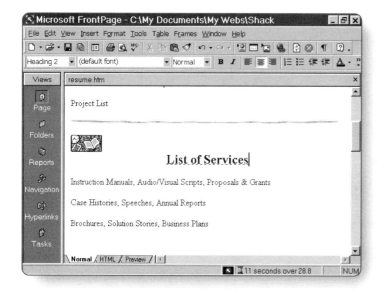

On text, bookmarks are indicated by a dashed underline.

7. **Create** any **additional bookmarks** that you want to include on the same page. Now that you have created the bookmarks, it is time to create the hyperlinks that will take your visitors to them.

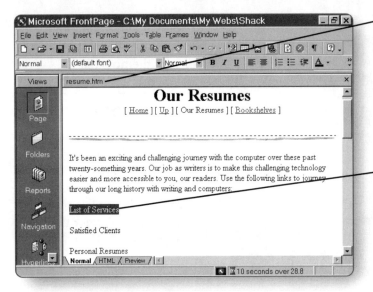

8. Open the **page** that will contain the hyperlink to the bookmark. This can be the same page in which you placed the bookmarks or a different page. The page will appear in the Page view window.

9. Select the **text or graphic** that you want to use as the link. The text or graphic will be highlighted.

10. Click on the **Hyperlink button**. The Create Hyperlink dialog box will appear.

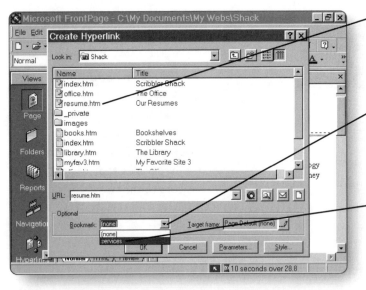

11. Click on the **page** containing the bookmark to which you want to create a link. The page will be selected.

12. Click on the **down arrow** next to the Bookmark list box. A list of bookmarks contained on that page will appear.

13. Click on the **bookmark** to which you want to link. The bookmark will be selected.

14. Click on **OK**. The hyperlink to the bookmark will be created.

Linking to Files

If you have a specific file that you want your visitors to use, such as a Microsoft Word, Excel, or PowerPoint file, create a hyperlink that leads them to it. When you create a link to one of these files, the visitor's Web browser will open the associated application (if it is installed on their computer) or open a viewer so that your visitors can view and print these files. Before you can create links to these files, you'll need to import them into your Web site's file structure.

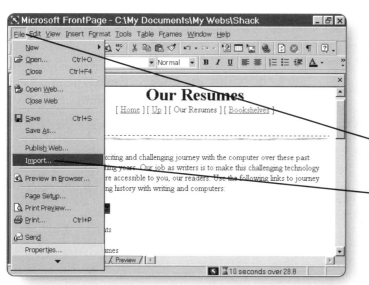

1. Click on **File**. The File menu will appear.

2. Click on **Import**. The Import dialog box will open.

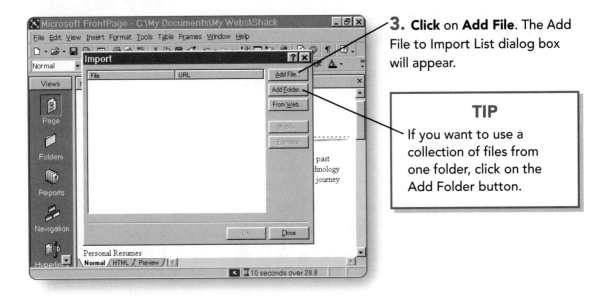

3. Click on **Add File**. The Add File to Import List dialog box will appear.

TIP

If you want to use a collection of files from one folder, click on the Add Folder button.

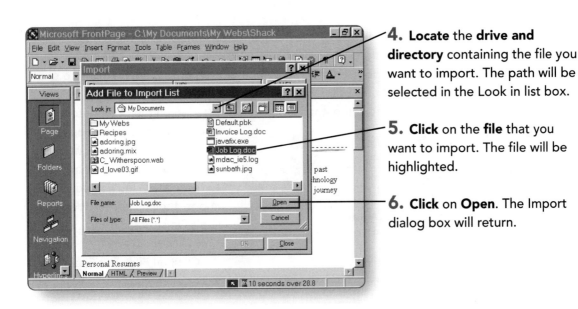

4. Locate the **drive and directory** containing the file you want to import. The path will be selected in the Look in list box.

5. Click on the **file** that you want to import. The file will be highlighted.

6. Click on **Open**. The Import dialog box will return.

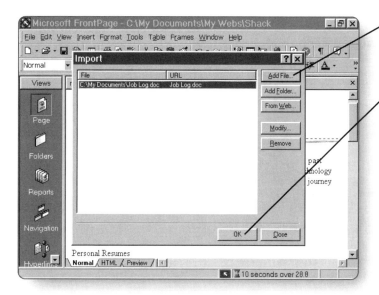

7. Add any **additional files** that you want to use in your Web site.

8. Click on **OK**. These files will be added to the Folder List for the Web site.

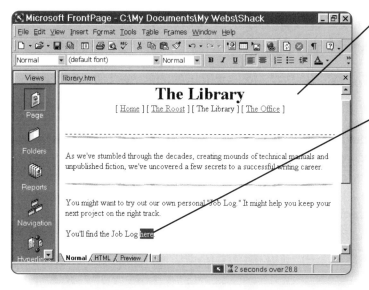

9. Open the **page** that will contain the hyperlink to the file. The page will appear in the Page view window.

10. Select the **text or graphic** that you want to use as the link. The text or graphic will be highlighted.

11. Click on the **Hyperlink button**. The Create Hyperlink dialog box will appear.

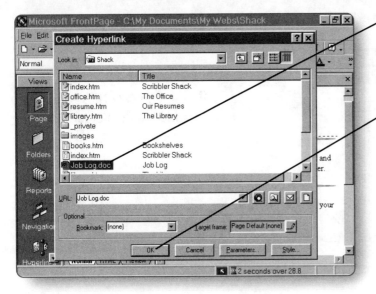

12. Click on the **file** that you just imported and to which you want to create the link. The file will be selected.

13. Click on **OK**. The hyperlink to the file will be created.

Creating Links to Pages on the Web

If you have a favorite Web site that you want to share with your visitors, you can make it easy for them by creating a hyperlink. Before you create a hyperlink to a Web site, you should check with the owner of the site and ask permission to link. You can find out if they are willing to do this by looking through the Web site or by sending a short e-mail message. Most Web site owners will gladly comply with your request, but some may have restrictions.

NOTE

Make sure you are connected to the Internet before you begin.

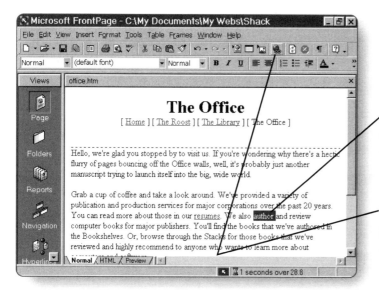

1. Open the **page** that will contain the link to another Web site. The page will appear in the Page view window.

2. Select the **text or graphic** that you want to use as the link. The text or graphic will be highlighted.

3. Click on the **Hyperlink button**. The Create Hyperlink dialog box will appear.

TIP

The easiest way to create a hyperlink is to type the URL address on your Web page just as if you were typing text. FrontPage will automatically turn the text into a link.

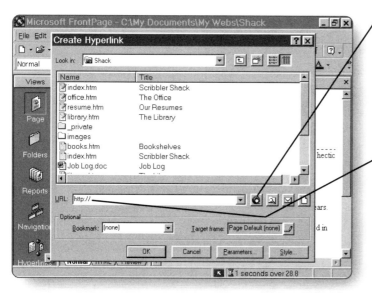

4. Click on the **Use your Web browser to select a page or file button**. Your default Web browser will open.

TIP

If you know the URL address of the Web page to which you want to create the hyperlink, type the address in the URL text box.

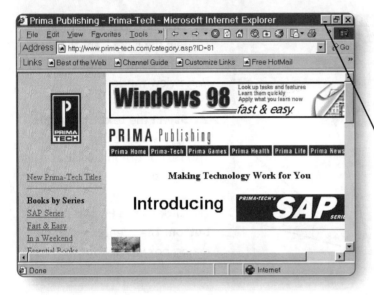

5. Using your Web browser, **locate** the **Web page** to which you want to create the link. The Web page will appear in the browser window.

6. **Click** on the **Minimize button**. The Create Hyperlink dialog box will return with the address of the Web page in the URL text box.

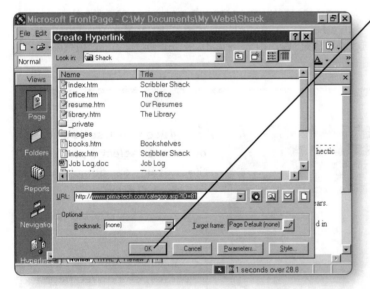

7. **Click** on **OK**. The hyperlink will be created.

TIP

If one of your Web pages contains numerous Web links or it contains a link to another Web site with many hyperlink options, you may want to add a note to the page reminding visitors to use the Back button on their browser to return to your site.

Creating E-mail Links

E-mail hyperlinks make it easy for your visitors to contact you. When a visitor clicks on the e-mail link, his or her default e-mail program will start, open a new message window, and enter your e-mail address in the "To" field. Your visitors simply type a message and press the Send button.

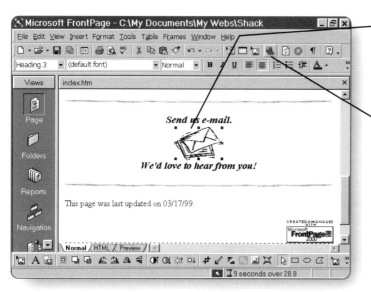

1. Select the **text or graphic** to which you want to create the e-mail hyperlink. The text or graphic will be highlighted.

2. Click on the **Hyperlink button**. The Create Hyperlink dialog box will open.

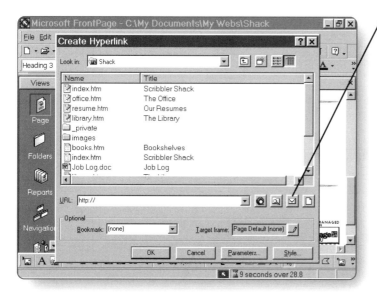

3. Click on the **Make a hyperlink that sends E-mail button**. The Create E-mail Hyperlink dialog box will open.

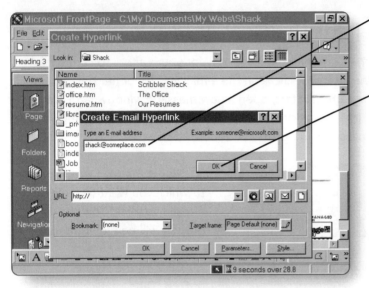

4. **Type** the **e-mail address** to which you want visitors' e-mail delivered.

5. **Click** on **OK**. The Create Hyperlink dialog box will return, showing the e-mail hyperlink in the URL text box.

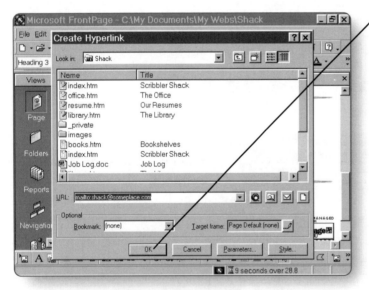

6. **Click** on **OK**. The e-mail hyperlink will be created.

Making Changes to Hyperlinks

Once a hyperlink has been created, it's easy to change the address of the page to which the link points.

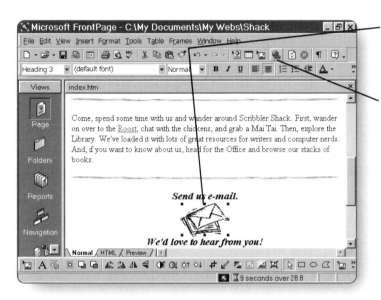

1. Click on the **hyperlink** that you want to edit. The hyperlink will be selected.

2. Click on the **Hyperlink button**. The Edit Hyperlink dialog box will appear.

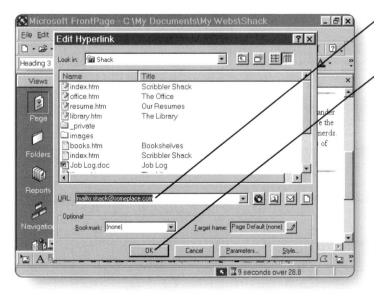

3. Make any **changes** as needed.

4. Click on **OK**. The hyperlink will be updated.

Selecting Hyperlink Colors

You can change the color scheme that is used to display hyperlinks. Visitors use these colors to determine whether they have previously visited the various links. When you set hyperlink colors, you do so for only one page in your Web site. You'll need to change each page to make them consistent and to reduce confusion for your visitors.

NOTE

If you are using one of the FrontPage themes, you will need to modify the hyperlink colors from the Themes dialog box.

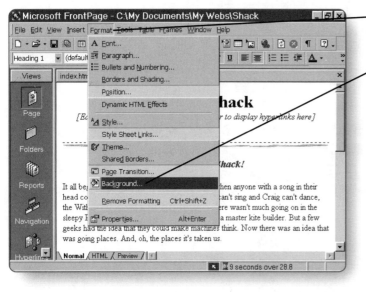

1. **Click** on **Format**. The Format menu will appear.

2. **Click** on **Background**. The Page Properties dialog box will appear with the Background tab on top.

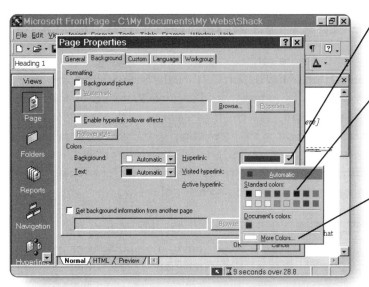

3. **Click** on the **down arrow** next to the Hyperlink list box. A selection of colors will appear.

4. **Click** on a **color**. The color will show in the list box.

NOTE

Choose additional colors by clicking on More Colors.

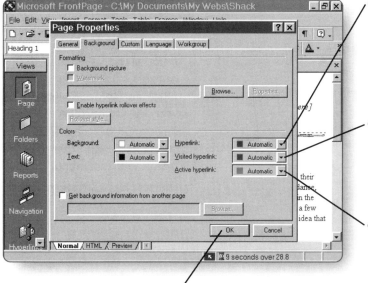

- **Hyperlink**. This setting determines the color displayed when a visitor to the Web site has not yet accessed the page specified by the link.

- **Visited hyperlink**. This setting determines the color displayed after a visitor has accessed the page specified by the link.

- **Active hyperlink**. This setting determines the color displayed when a visitor clicks on the hyperlink.

5. **Click** on **OK**. The new color scheme will be applied to the Web page.

Setting Navigation Elements

One of the more confusing aspects of designing a Web site is the addition of navigation buttons that help visitors find their way around. If you had to add each navigation control to each page individually, you could easily miss a link or you could link a navigation button to the wrong page. If your visitors can't navigate your site correctly, they'll lose interest and find another site. FrontPage takes the hassle out of building navigation controls by doing most of the work for you.

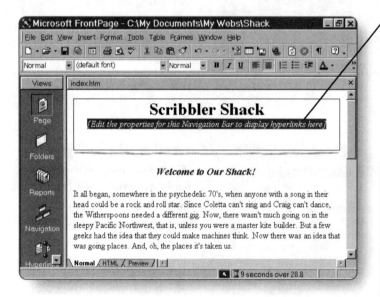

1. Double-click on the **navigation buttons** or the navigation placeholder contained inside a shared border. The Navigation Bar Properties dialog box will appear.

NOTE

If you aren't using shared borders, click on the place on the page where you want to add the navigation buttons. Then select Navigation Bar from the Insert menu.

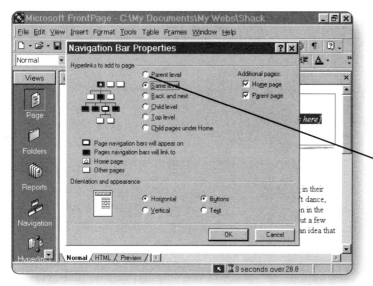

2. Click on one of the **option buttons** from the Hyperlinks to add to page section of the dialog box. Choose the option that corresponds to the page level you want to display in the Navigation bar:

- **Parent level** displays navigation controls to the pages that are above the selected page in the Navigation chart.

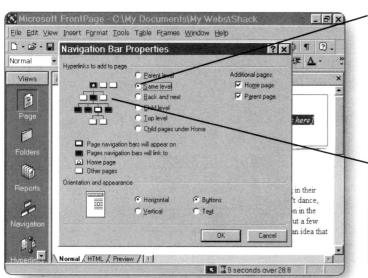

- **Same level** displays navigation controls to the pages that are on the same level as the selected page in the Navigation chart.

NOTE

Use the diagram at the left of the option buttons to help determine which pages will appear as links in the Navigation Bar.

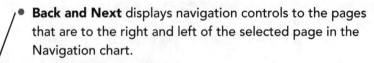

Back and Next displays navigation controls to the pages that are to the right and left of the selected page in the Navigation chart.

Child level displays navigation controls to the pages that are below the selected page in the Navigation chart.

Top level displays navigation controls to the pages that link the selected page to the Home Page. This also displays links to the Home Page and any other pages at the Home Page level.

Child pages under Home displays those pages that are on the level directly below the Home page in the Navigation chart.

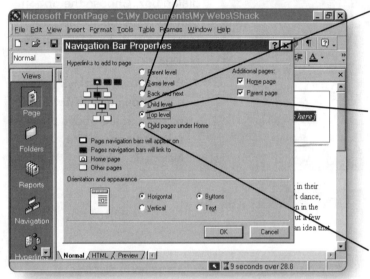

3. **Click** on **Home page** to add a navigation button that directs visitors to your Home Page. A check will appear in the box.

4. **Click** on **Parent page** to add a navigation button that directs visitors to the page above the selected page. A check will appear in the box.

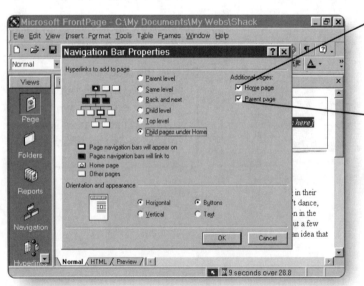

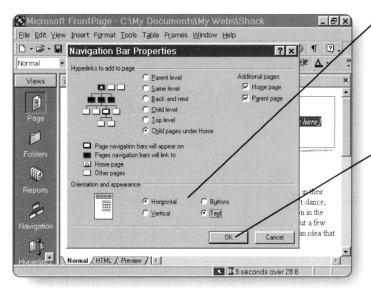

5. **Click** on an **option button** to select the orientation of the navigation controls. The option will be selected, and the preview to the left will change accordingly.

6. **Click** on **OK**.

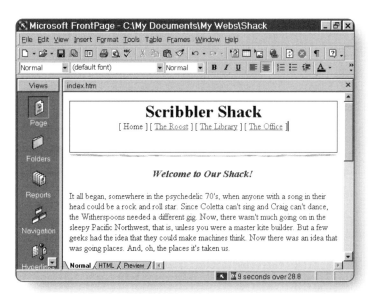

The Navigation Bar will be updated on the page. If you are using shared borders, the Navigation bar will be updated on all the pages of your site.

TIP

To add a plain, gray, horizontal line to your Web page, select Horizontal Line from the Insert menu.

7

Creating and Formatting Lists

You can find lists in almost every part of your daily life. At home, you put together to-do lists and grocery lists. At work, the boss may hand out an agenda before a meeting or you may read a procedure manual that lists the steps it takes to perform a task. On the Internet, you'll find lists on some of the Web pages that you visit. FrontPage makes it easy to format several different types of lists. In this chapter, you'll learn how to:

- Create and edit simple lists
- Create numbered and nested lists
- Format different list types
- Build collapsible lists
- Replace plain list bullets with creative graphics

Creating Simple Lists

You can create two types of simple lists in FrontPage: bulleted lists and numbered lists. A bulleted list is simply a group of unordered items. A numbered list consists of items that must be in a particular order, such as steps required to perform a task. This section will show you how to format a simple bulleted list and how to add items after the list has been created.

1. Open the **page** where the list will be located. The page will appear in the Page view window.

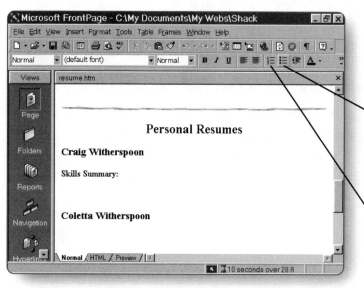

2. Click on the **place** where you want the list to begin. The insertion bar (the cursor) will appear in the selected area.

3a. Click on the **Bullets button**. A bullet will appear before the insertion point.

OR

3b. Click on the **Numbering button**. The number 1 will appear before the insertion point.

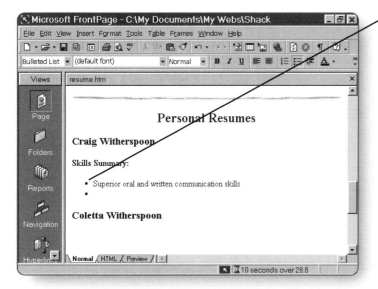

4. Type a **list item** and **press the Enter key**. The insertion point will move to the next line and another bullet or number will appear.

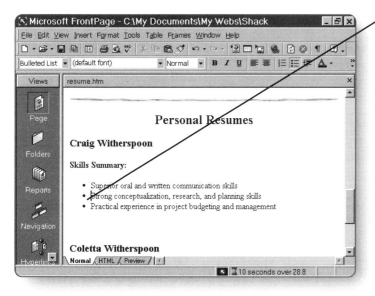

5. Type the remaining **list items**.

6. Press the **Enter key twice** at the end of the final list item.

TIP

To convert normal text to a list, select the paragraphs that you want formatted as a list and click on the Bulleted List or Numbered List button.

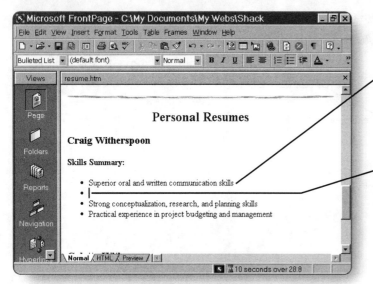

Inserting an Item into an Existing List

1. Click on the end of the **line** that will precede the new list item. The insertion bar will appear in the selected place.

2. Press the **Enter key**. A blank line will appear as the next list entry.

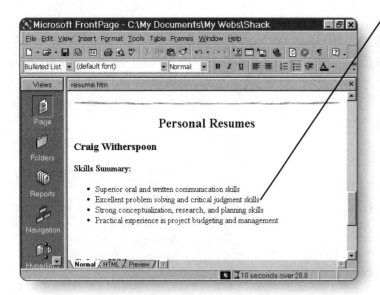

3. Type the new **list item** in this blank line. Do not press Enter unless you want to add another list item.

TIP

To create a list within a list, select the list item that you want to indent and click on the Increase Indent button.

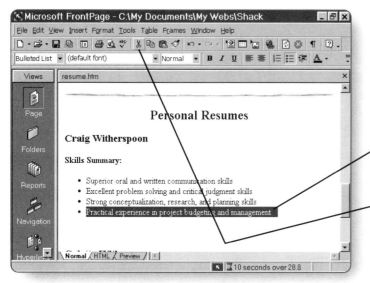

Deleting an Item from the List

1. Place the **mouse pointer** over the bullet in front of the item you want to delete.

2. Click on the **bullet**. The item will be selected.

3. Click on the **Cut button**. The item will be deleted.

NOTE
You can use the Copy and Paste buttons to move and copy list items.

Creating an Ordered List

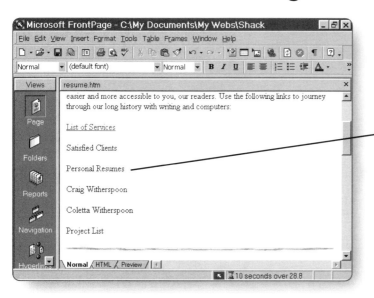

Ordered lists are just as easy to build, format, and edit as bulleted lists. FrontPage gives you some control over how these lists can be organized.

1. Type the **list items** in the order that you want them to appear in the list.

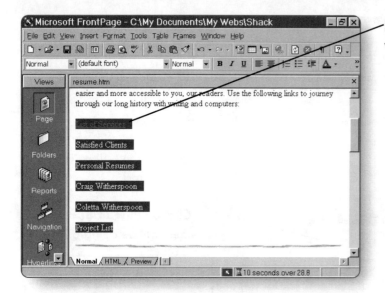

2. Select the entire **list**. The list will be highlighted.

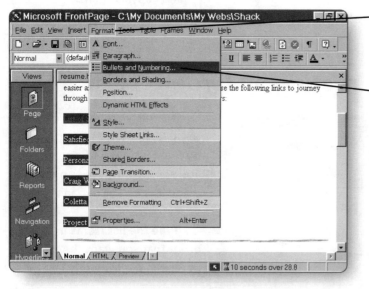

3. Click on **Format** on the menu bar. The Format menu will appear.

4. Click on **Bullets and Numbering**. The Bullets and Numbering dialog box will open.

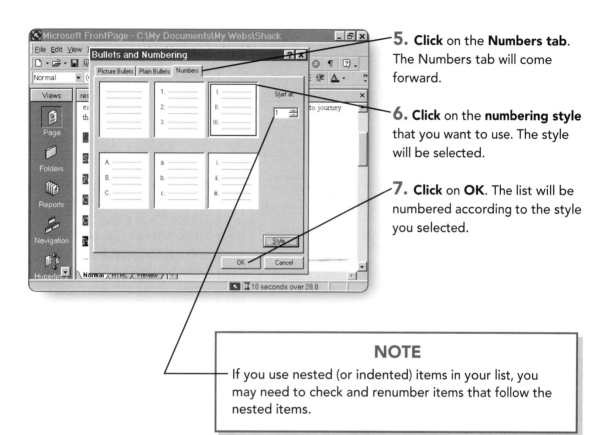

5. Click on the **Numbers tab**. The Numbers tab will come forward.

6. Click on the **numbering style** that you want to use. The style will be selected.

7. Click on **OK**. The list will be numbered according to the style you selected.

NOTE

If you use nested (or indented) items in your list, you may need to check and renumber items that follow the nested items.

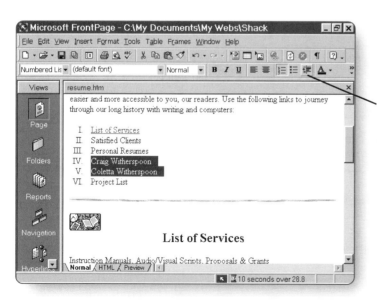

8. Select the **item(s)** that you want nested in the list. The item or items will be highlighted.

9. Click on the **Increase Indent** button. The items will be indented.

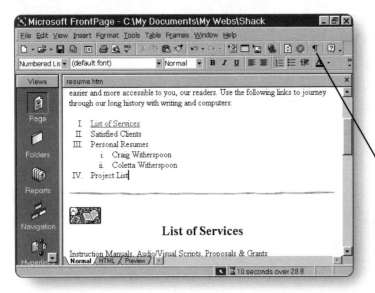

If you want to change the numbering scheme for nested items, select them and change the numbering style from the Bullets and Numbering dialog box.

NOTE

To see paragraph markers in the Page view, click on the Show All button. Click on the Show All button a second time to hide paragraph markers.

Using Styles to Format Lists

With FrontPage, you are not limited to simple bulleted and ordered lists. You can also create directory lists, short menus, and definition lists (which usually list single terms followed by descriptive paragraphs). To format one of these lists, you will need to apply a style to the list.

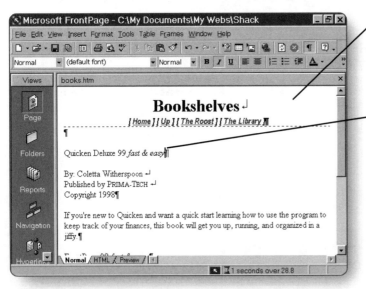

1. Open the **page** where the list will be located. The page will appear in the Page view window.

2. Click on the **place** where you want the list to begin. The pointer will appear in the selected place.

3. Type the **list items**.

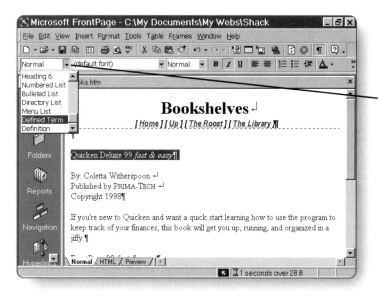

4. Select the **list items** to be formatted. The items will be highlighted.

5. Click on the **down arrow** to the right of the Style field. A drop-down list of styles will appear.

6. Click on the **style** you want to apply to the list items. The style will be applied.

- **Defined Term.** This style is used in conjunction with the Definition style to create definition lists. Definition lists consist of specific terms followed by their definitions. Place the word to be defined on the line above the definition. Defined terms appear against the left margin.

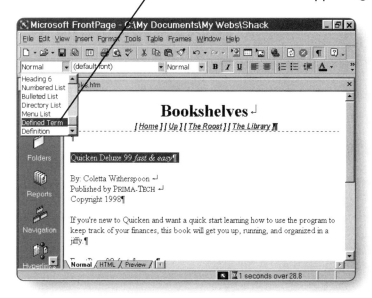

- **Definition**. This style is used in conjunction with the Defined Term style. Place the definition on the line below the word being defined. Definitions are indented away from the left margin.

- **Directory List**. A directory list is a sequence of short terms.

- **Menu List**. A menu list contains an unordered list of short entries.

Building Collapsible Lists

In the past, knowledge of Java or ActiveX programming was required to build a list that would expand and collapse when a visitor clicked on it. With FrontPage, you can rely on the collapsible list feature to build the Dynamic HTML code for these lists. No special programming skills are required.

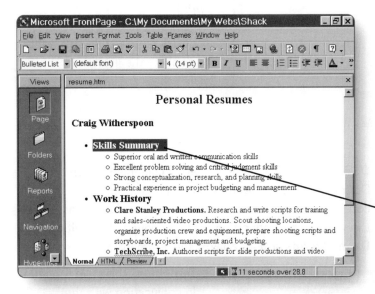

1. Open the **page** that will contain your collapsible list. The page will appear in the Page view window.

2. Type and format the **list** items. You can use any of the list formats discussed earlier in the chapter to format your list.

3. Select the **level** in the list below which you want to enable the collapsible feature. Only those items that are nested under this level will be collapsible. The level will be selected.

4. Right-click on the **item** that you want to collapse. A shortcut menu will appear.

5. Click on **List Properties**. The List Properties dialog box will open.

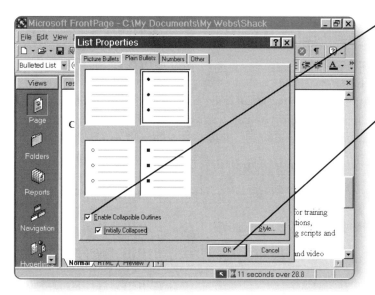

6. Click in the **Enable Collapsible Outlines** check box. A check mark will appear in the box.

7. Click on **OK**. The collapsible outline feature will be applied at the specified level.

> ### NOTE
> Click in the Initially Collapsed check box if you want the nested items to be hidden when your visitors first see this page in their Web browsers.

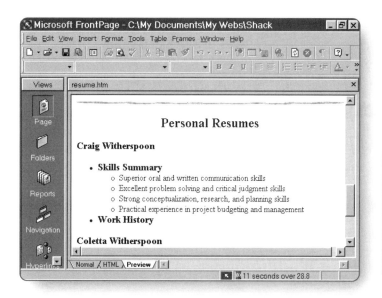

> ### NOTE
> To see your collapsible list in action, you'll need to preview the page in a Web browser that supports Dynamic HTML, such as Microsoft Internet Explorer version 4 or higher. If you can't remember how to preview your pages, see "Previewing from a Web Browser" in Chapter 5.

Adding Graphical Bullets

If you created your Web site using one of the FrontPage themes, you'll notice that all of your bulleted lists are formatted with graphical bullets. You aren't limited to just these bullets, and you can add your own flair by replacing the bullets with your own graphics. If you aren't using a theme to create your Web site, format the list and change the plain bullet character to any image you like.

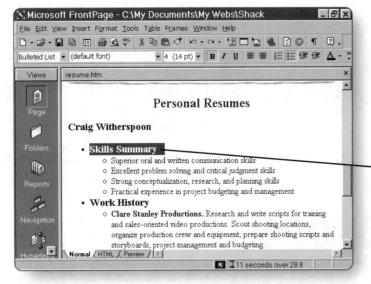

1. Open the **page** that contains the bulleted list that you'd like to spice up. The page will appear in the Page view window.

2. Click on the bullet next to the level within the list to which you want to change the bullet style. The item next to the bullet will be highlighted.

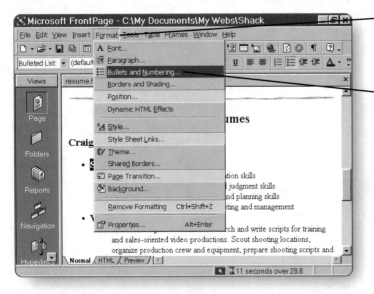

3. Click on **Format** on the menu bar. The Format menu will appear.

4. Click on **Bullets and Numbering**. The List Properties dialog box will appear.

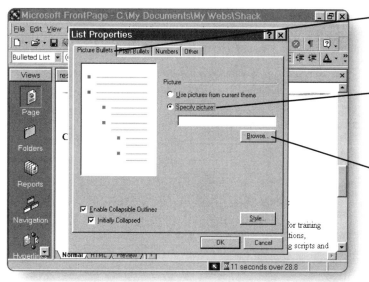

5. **Click** on the **Picture Bullets tab**. The Picture Bullets tab will come forward.

6. **Click** on the **Specify picture option button**. The option will be selected.

7. **Click** on **Browse**. The Select Picture dialog box will open.

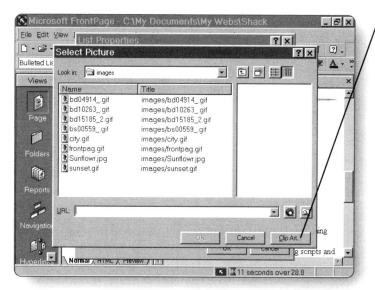

8. **Click** on **Clip Art**. The Clip Art Gallery dialog box will appear.

TIP

If you want to use an image stored on your computer, click on the Select a File on Your Computer button. You'll learn more about this in Chapter 9, "Working with Graphics."

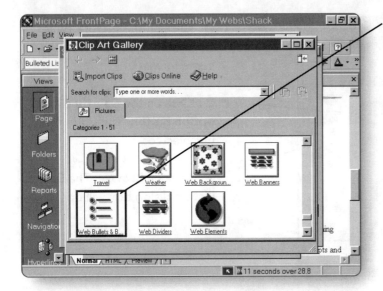

9. Click on a **category**. A list of clip art images will appear.

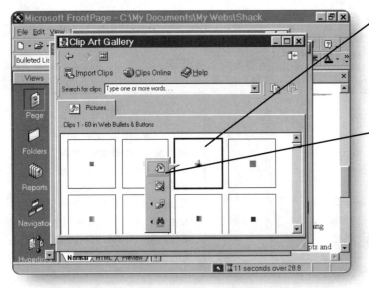

10. Click on the **clip art** that you want to use for the bullet. The image will be highlighted, and a list of option buttons will open.

11. Click on **Insert clip**. The List Properties dialog box will return with the image path displayed in the Specify picture text box.

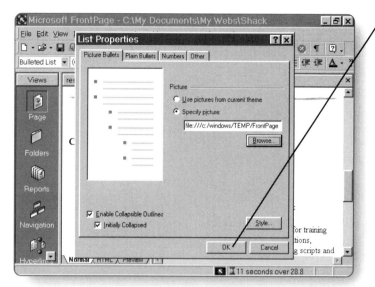

12. Click on **OK**. The bullets will change to the new bullet you selected.

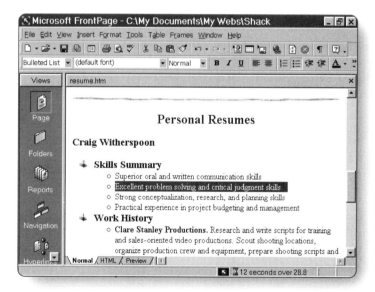

TIP

If you are using nested items in your list, you'll want to use a different bullet graphic to set these items apart from the main list.

8

Creating and Formatting Tables

You've probably seen tables used in spreadsheets and word processing documents. Tables are a great way to organize information. Tables are especially useful in Web pages because you can't use the Tab key to create orderly columns of information. The best way to get around this obstacle is to use a table. Tables are also helpful when you want to place text and graphics side by side. In this chapter, you'll learn how to:

- Create a simple table
- Place text and images into a cell
- Add color to your table
- Change the display size of a table
- Set the width of table rows
- Convert text into table format

Creating a Table

Before you begin building tables, you may want to display the Tables toolbar. The Tables toolbar will help you build and edit tables quickly and efficiently.

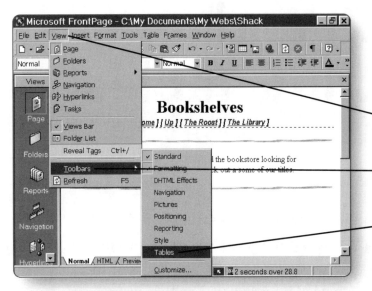

1. Open the **page** on which you want to create a table. The page will appear in the Page view window.

2. Click on **View** on the menu bar. The View menu will appear.

3. Click on **Toolbars**. A second menu will appear.

4. Click on **Tables**. The Tables toolbar will display as a floating toolbar.

5. Click and hold the **mouse pointer** on the toolbar's title bar, **drag** the **toolbar** to the desired location on your screen, and **release** the **mouse button**. You may want to place the Table toolbar below the other toolbars at the top of the program window. The toolbar will be moved.

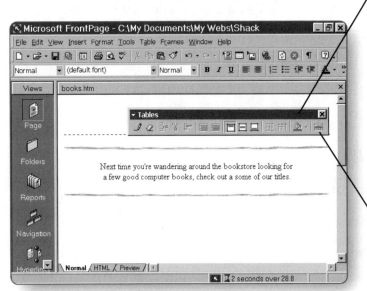

NOTE

The buttons on the Table toolbar are grayed-out if the insertion bar (the cursor) is not located inside the table.

Creating the Border

You should have an approximate idea of the size of the table you want. If you aren't exactly sure, don't worry. You can always add, delete, and merge rows and columns later.

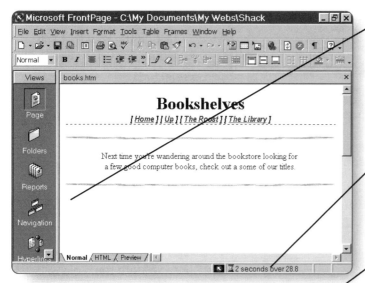

1. **Click** on the **place** where you want to insert the table. The insertion bar (the cursor) will appear in the selected position.

TIP

The Status Bar tells you how long it will take your Web site visitors to download the page.

---

2. **Click** on the **Insert Table button**. A table palette will appear.

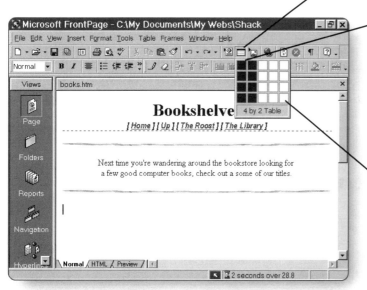

3. **Click and hold** the **mouse button** on the upper left cell of the table palette. The table size will appear at the bottom of the table palette showing you the number of rows and columns that will be created.

4. **Drag** the **mouse pointer** down and to the right. The table size will grow.

5. **Release** the **mouse button** when the table is the desired size. A blank table will appear on the page.

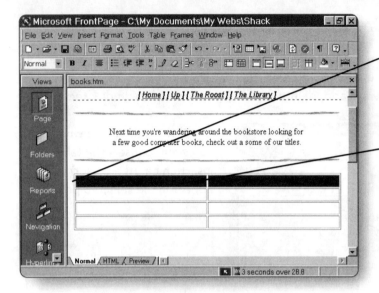

Adding Rows

1. Place the **mouse pointer** along the left edge of the table. The mouse pointer will change to a right-pointing arrow.

2. Click on the **row** that will follow the new row. The row will be selected.

TIP

To add multiple rows at one time, select several rows by clicking on the first row and dragging the mouse pointer over the other rows you want to select. The number of rows inserted into the table will be the same as the number of rows selected.

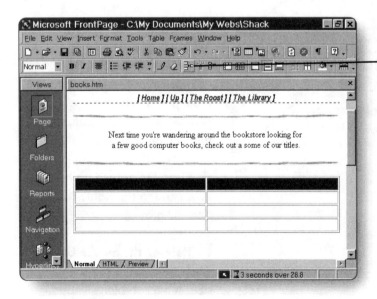

3. Click on the **Insert Rows button**. A new row will be added to the table and will appear above the selected row.

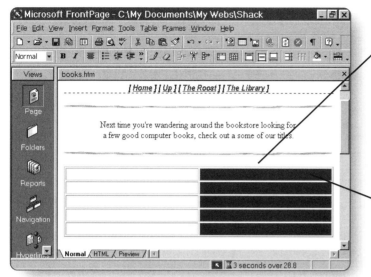

Adding Columns

1. Place the **mouse pointer** along the top edge of the table so that it is above the column that will be to the right of the new column. The mouse pointer will change to a down-pointing arrow.

2. Click on that **column**. The column will be selected.

NOTE

The Insert Rows or Columns command on the Table menu gives you more control when adding rows and columns.

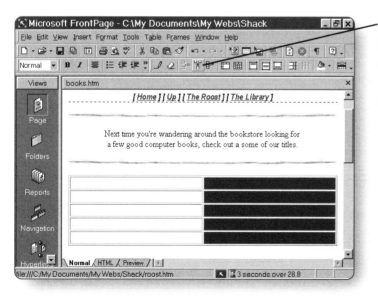

3. Click on the **Insert Columns button**. A new column will be added to the table and will appear to the left of the selected column.

Merging Cells

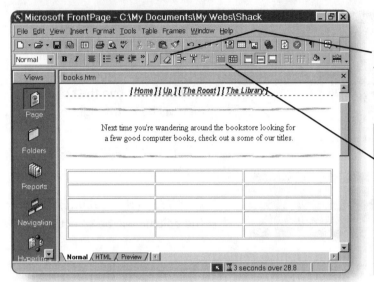

1. **Click** on the **Eraser button**. The mouse pointer will turn into an eraser.

NOTE

You can also merge and split cells by selecting the cells with which you want to work and then clicking on the Merge Cells and Split Cells buttons.

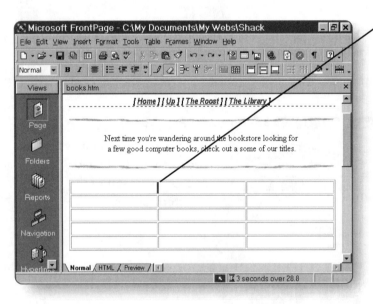

2. To combine two cells within a row, **click and hold** the **mouse button** to the left of the vertical cell border between the two cells that you want to merge.

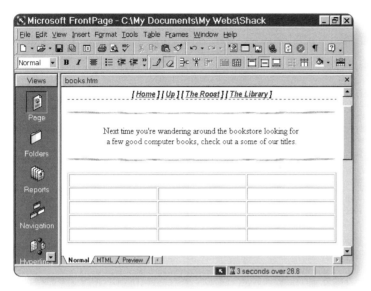

3. **Drag** the **mouse pointer** to the right and across the cell border. The cell border will be selected.

4. **Release** the **mouse button**. The selected cell border will disappear and the two cells will be merged.

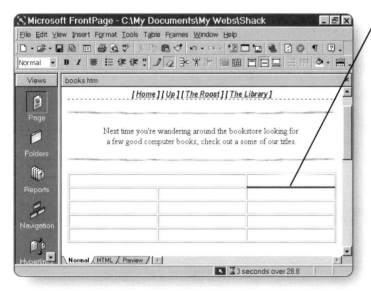

5. To combine two cells within a column, **click and hold** the **mouse button** above the cell border between the two cells that you want to merge.

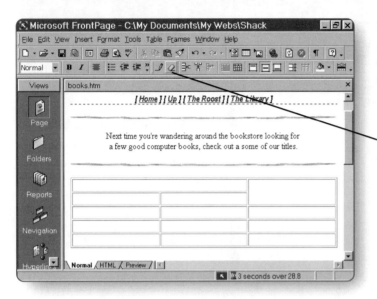

6. Drag the **mouse pointer** down and across the cell border. The cell border will be selected. When you release the mouse button, the two cells will merge.

7. Click on the **Eraser button** to turn off the merge function.

Changing the Column Width

You'll notice that, initially, the columns in your table are of equal width. You can change the width of columns to fit your needs.

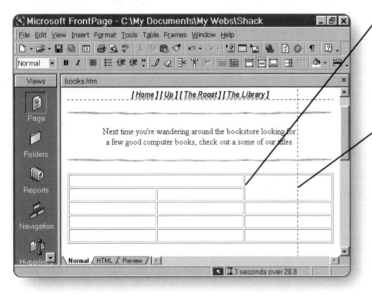

1. Position the **mouse pointer** on the line between the two columns that you want to change. The mouse pointer will turn into a double arrowhead.

2. Press and hold the **mouse button** and **drag** the **line** to the left or to the right to change the size of the columns.

3. Release the **mouse button**. The width of the two columns will be altered according to your placement of the dividing line.

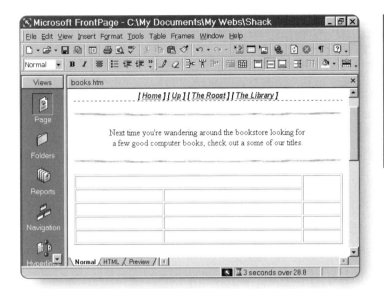

TIP

You can change the row height by positioning the mouse pointer on a line and holding the mouse button while dragging up or down.

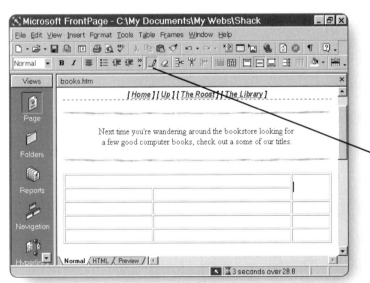

Using the Drawing Tools to Add Cells

You can easily add a new cell or an additional row or column to your table.

1. Click on the **Draw Table button**. The mouse pointer will turn into a pencil.

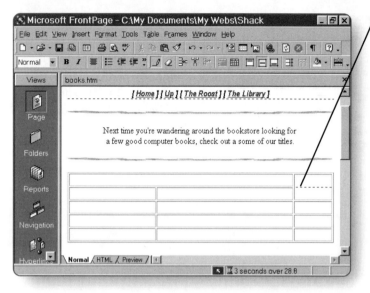

2. Press and hold the **mouse button** where you want place the new cell.

3. Drag the **mouse pointer** to the location where you want to end the new cell.

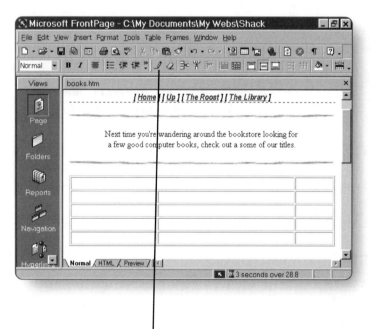

4. Release the **mouse button**. A new cell will be added to the table.

TIP

To create a new column, click at the top of the table where you want to add a new column and drag the mouse pointer to the bottom of the table. Create a new row by dragging the mouse from the right to the left side of the table.

---

5. Click on the **Draw Table button**. The drawing feature will be turned off.

Adding a Caption

If you want to leave your visitors a message about the contents of the table, add a caption.

1. Click anywhere inside the **table**. The insertion bar will appear in the table.

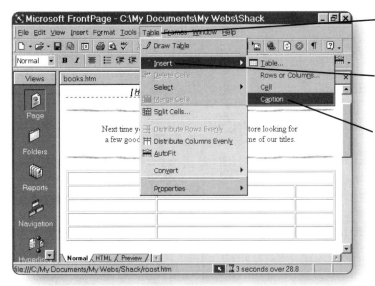

2. Click on **Table** on the menu bar. The Table menu will appear.

3. Click on **Insert**. A second menu will appear.

4. Click on **Caption**. The insertion bar will appear above the table.

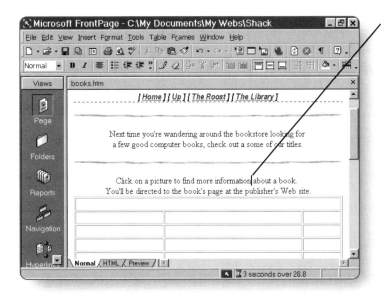

5. Type a **caption** for the table.

Inserting Content into a Cell

After you have built a structure for your table, you can begin to add some words and pictures.

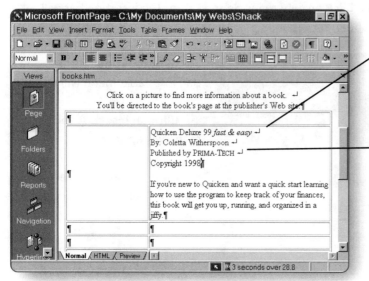

Adding Text

1. Click in the **cell** where you want to place the text. The insertion bar will appear in the cell.

2. Type the **text**.

TIP

To add a second row of text in a separate paragraph, press the Enter key. To add new lines within a single paragraph, press Shift+Enter.

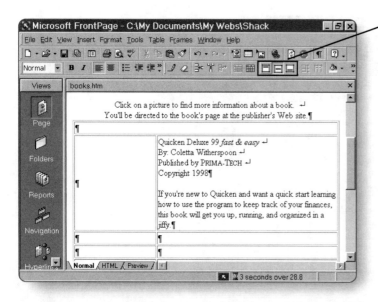

3. Click on a **paragraph position button** on the Tables toolbar. The text will be aligned in the cell.

- **Align Top** places the text at the top of the cell.

- **Center Vertically** places the text in the middle of the cell.

- **Align Bottom** places the text at the bottom of the cell.

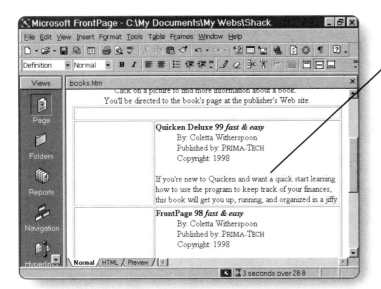

NOTE

You can format text the same way you would in any other place on a Web page. Use the formatting toolbar, the style list, or the format menu commands to transform your text.

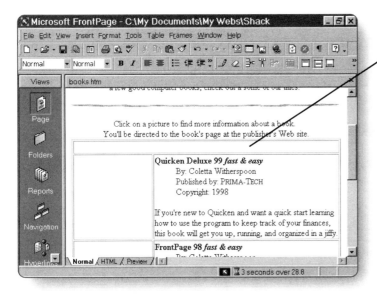

Adding Images

1. Click in the **cell** in which you want to place the image. The insertion bar will appear in the cell.

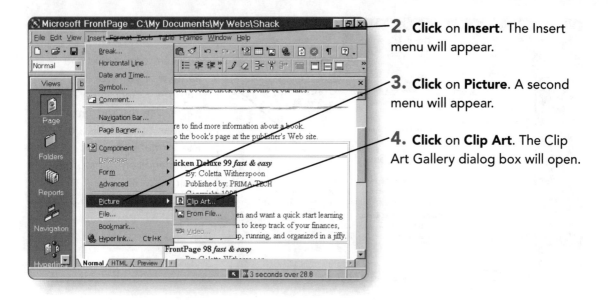

2. Click on **Insert**. The Insert menu will appear.

3. Click on **Picture**. A second menu will appear.

4. Click on **Clip Art**. The Clip Art Gallery dialog box will open.

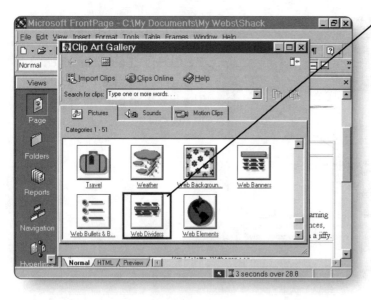

5. Click on a **category**. A list of clip art images will appear.

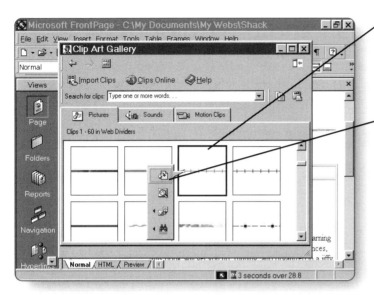

6. **Click** on the clip art **image** that you want to insert into the table. A list of option buttons will appear.

7. **Click** on **Insert clip**. The image will appear in the cell.

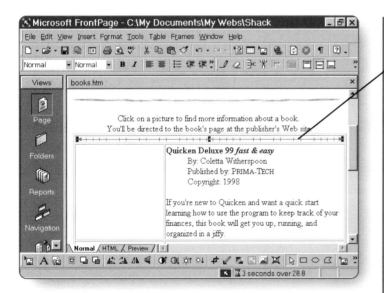

TIP

You can change the size of the inserted image by clicking on it to display the image handles. Click and hold an image handle while you move the mouse pointer away from the image to make it larger, or toward the image to make it smaller. To learn more about working with images, see Chapter 9, "Working with Graphics."

Changing the Color of a Cell

After you have created a table and added text and graphics, you may decide that the table lacks color. You can spruce up your tables by adding background colors.

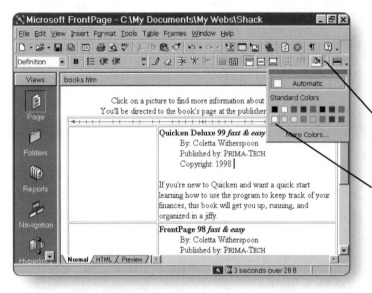

1. Click on the **cell** in which you want to change the background color. The insertion bar will appear in the cell.

2. Click on the **Fill Color button**. A color palette will appear.

3. Click on a **color**.

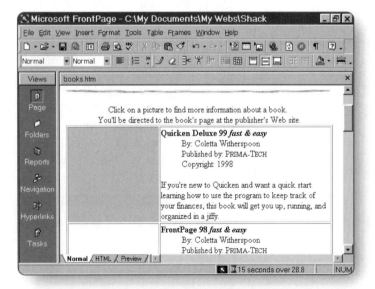

The color will fill the background of the selected cell.

Controlling the Size of the Table

You have several options when deciding how your table will display in your visitor's Web browser. You can create a table that always fits within the browser window. This way your visitors don't have to scroll back and forth to read the information. However, if your information needs a specific amount of space in which to display, you may want to fix the size of the table.

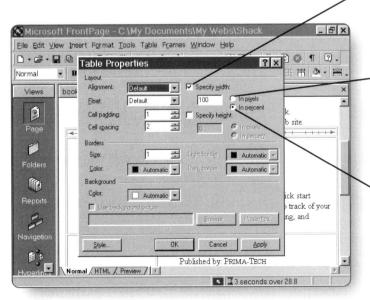

1. **Click** on **Table** on the menu bar. The Table menu will appear.

2. **Click** on **Properties**. A second menu will appear.

3. **Click** on **Table**. The Table Properties dialog box will open.

4. **Click** in the **Specify width check box,** if it is not already selected. A check will appear in the box.

5a. **Click** on the **In pixels option button** if you want to set a specific width for your table. The option will be selected.

OR

5b. **Click** on the **In percent option button** if you want the width of your table to span a certain percentage of the visitor's browser window. The option will be selected.

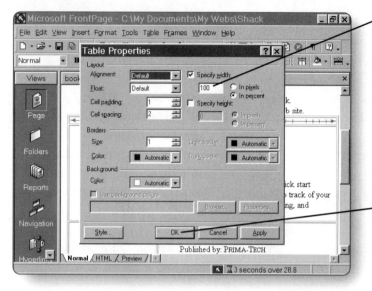

6. Click in the **Specify width text box** and **type** a **number**. If you selected the In percent option button and you want the table to span the entire width of the browser window, type 100. If you selected the In pixels option button, type the number of pixels.

7. Click on **OK**. The display width will be applied to your table.

Setting Row Widths

You can set up rows to display as a certain percent of the entire screen width or as a set number of pixels.

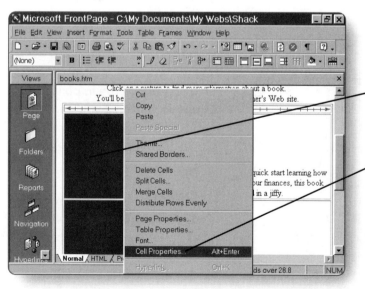

1. Select all the **cells** in the row that you want to change the width. The row will be selected.

2. Right-click on a **cell** in the row for which you want to set the width. A menu will appear.

3. Click on **Cell Properties**. The Cell Properties dialog box will open.

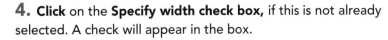

4. **Click** on the **Specify width check box,** if this is not already selected. A check will appear in the box.

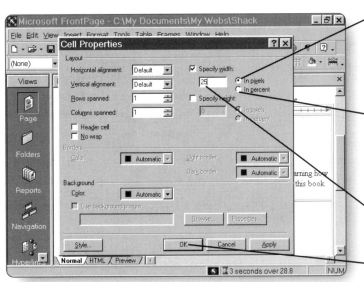

5a. **Click** on the **In pixels option button** to create a row that is a fixed number of pixels.

OR

5b. **Click** on the **In percent option button** to create a row that is a specified percent of the width of the viewer's screen.

6. **Click** in the **Specify width** text box and type a number.

7. **Click** on **OK**. The width will be applied to the entire row.

Converting Text into a Table

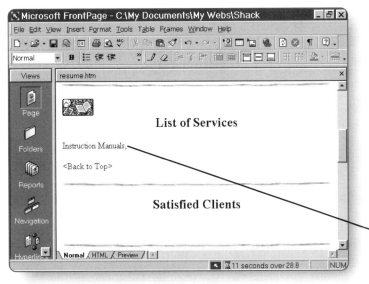

You can type the information that you want to place in a table before you build the table. By designing information in this order, you can leave it to FrontPage to automatically format the table to fit the text.

1. **Click** on the **place** where you want to start the table. The insertion bar will appear.

2. **Type** the **text** (followed by a comma) that you want to place in the first column of the first row.

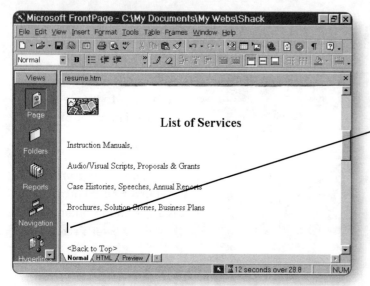

3. Type additional **entries** to be placed in the remaining columns of the row, each followed by a comma (except after the last entry).

4. Type the last **entry** for the row and **press** the **Enter key**. The insertion bar will appear on the next line.

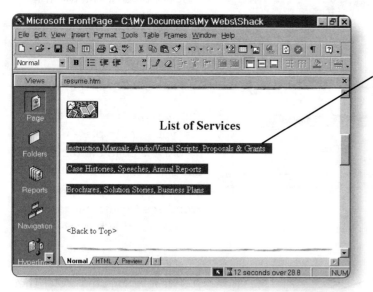

5. Add additional **rows** to the table as needed.

6. Select the **text** that you want to convert into a table. The text will be highlighted.

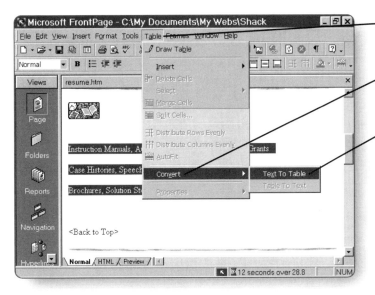

7. Click on **Table** on the menu bar. The Table menu will appear.

8. Click on **Convert**. A second menu will appear.

9. Click on **Text to Table**. The Convert Text to Table dialog box will open.

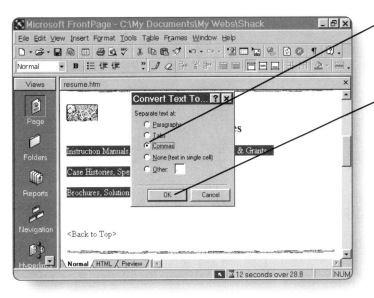

10. Click on the **Commas option button**. The option will be selected.

11. Click on **OK**. The text will appear inside a table.

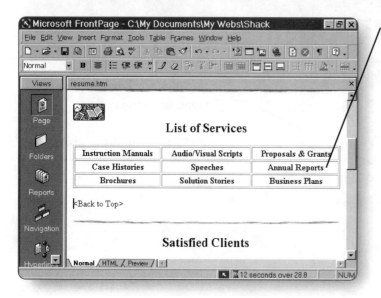

12. **Format** the **text and the table** to make it appealing.

Part III Review Questions

1. How can you direct a visitor to a certain place on a Web page?
    See "Creating Links to Bookmarks" in Chapter 6.

2. What are the two methods for creating a hyperlink to a page on the Internet? *See "Creating Links to Pages on the Web" in Chapter 6.*

3. Can the hyperlink colors used within a theme be changed?
    See "Selecting Hyperlink Colors" in Chapter 6.

4. What are the two types of simple lists that you can create on your Web pages? *See "Creating Simple Lists" in Chapter 7.*

5. Besides using toolbar buttons to format a list, what other method can you use? *See "Using Styles to Format Lists" in Chapter 7.*

6. How do you create a list where nested items can be hidden on a Web page? *See "Building Collapsible Lists" in Chapter 7.*

7. Can you use your own graphics as bullets instead of using FrontPage's default bullets? *See "Adding Graphical Bullets in Chapter 7.*

8. If you don't want to use the menu to create a table, where do you find a toolbar containing buttons that help you create and edit a table? *See "Creating a Table" in Chapter 8.*

9. How can you add several rows to a table in one quick and easy step? *See "Adding Rows" in Chapter 8.*

10. If you have text on a Web page, how can you convert this text into a table? *See "Converting Text into a Table" in Chapter 8.*

PART IV

Enhancing Your Web Site

9

Working with Graphics

Pictures are common on Web pages. Most Web images work best in one of two formats: JPEG or GIF. JPEG images include high-color pictures, such as scanned images of photographs. GIFs are pictures created in a computer drawing program, and they use only a few colors. GIF images can be stationary or animated. Pictures can do a lot to enhance your Web site, but make sure they are appropriate to the message that you want to convey to your visitors. In this chapter, you'll learn how to:

- Add pictures and graphics to your Web pages
- Display text around images
- Create hyperlinks using images
- Use images to enhance the page background

Inserting Images

There are a number of places where you can find artwork to place on your Web pages. The easiest place to find pictures is in the Clip Art Gallery provided by Microsoft. If you've had a chance to play with any of the graphics software programs, you may have created your own pictures that can be used in your Web pages.

Finding Clip Art

1. Open the **page** where you want to insert the clip art image. The page will open in the Page view window.

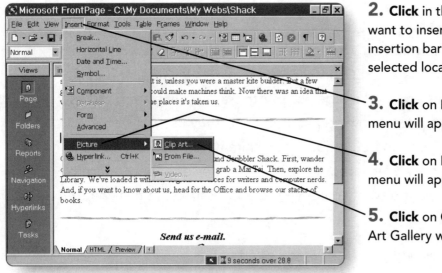

2. Click in the **place** where you want to insert the image. The insertion bar will appear in the selected location.

3. Click on **Insert**. The Insert menu will appear.

4. Click on **Picture**. A second menu will appear.

5. Click on **Clip Art**. The Clip Art Gallery will open.

TIP

If you have a scanner attached to your computer, you can scan images, import them into your Web site, and use them in your Web pages. Click on the Insert Picture from File button on the Standard toolbar.

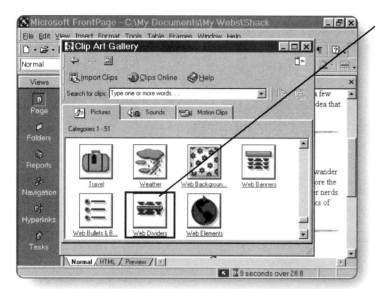

6. **Click** on a **category** of clip art that matches the type of image you want on your Web page. The images contained in the category will appear.

> ### NOTE
> If you don't know in which category an image may be located, type a few words to describe the image in the Search for clips text box.

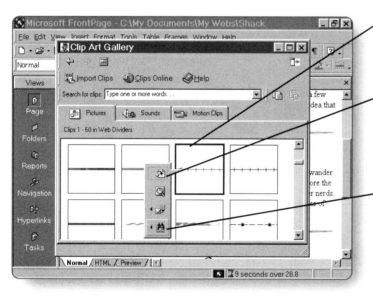

7. **Click** on the **image** that you want to add. A list of option buttons will appear.

8a. **Click** on **Insert clip**. The image will display on the Web page.

OR

8b. **Click** on **Find similar clips**. The list of option buttons will expand and a search function will appear.

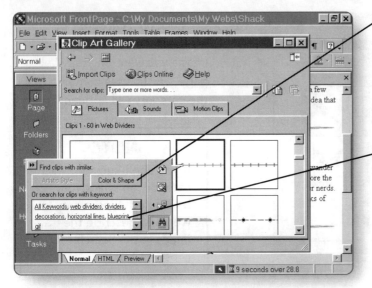

9a. Click on the **Color & Shape button**. All images in the Clip Art Gallery that are similar in color and shape to the selected image will appear.

OR

9b. Click on a **keyword hyperlink**. All images in the Clip Art Gallery that are associated with the selected keyword will appear.

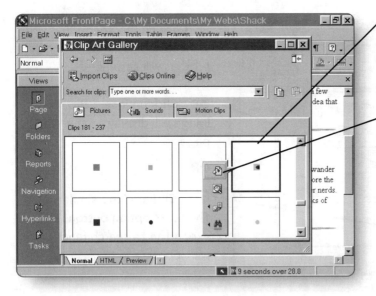

10. Click on the **image** that you want to add to the Web page. A list of option buttons will appear.

11. Click on **Insert clip**. The image will be placed on the Web page.

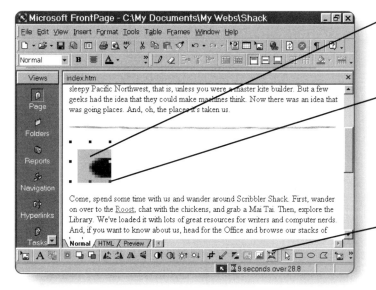

12. **Click** on the **new image** on the Web page. The image will be selected.

13. **Click and hold** one of the corner **image handles**, and then **drag** the **mouse pointer** toward the image to make it smaller or away from the image to make it larger. The image will be resized.

14. **Click** on the **Resample button**. The file size and quality of the image will be optimized.

TIP

You can move the Image Toolbar to a different location on your screen. Click and hold on the vertical bar at the left of the Image Toolbar. Drag the toolbar to a new location.

Adding Images to the Clip Art Gallery

All of the Microsoft Office programs use the Clip Art Gallery to manage graphic images. If you have an image that you want to make readily available, add it to the Clip Art Gallery. If you're looking for more clip art, there are images on Microsoft's Web site that you can add to the Clip Art Gallery easily.

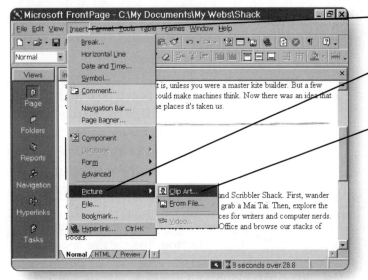

1. Click on **Insert**. The Insert menu will appear.

2. Click on **Picture**. A second menu will appear.

3. Click on **Clip Art**. The Clip Art Gallery will open.

NOTE

You can position an image on the page by using the paragraph alignment buttons.

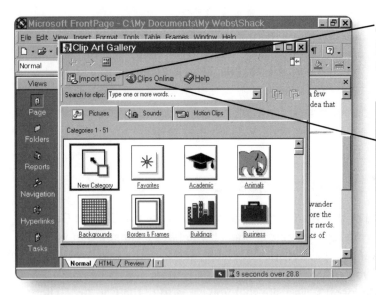

4. Click on the **Import Clips button**. The Add clip to Clip Gallery dialog box will appear.

TIP

The Clips Online button will connect you to the Internet and Microsoft's Web site. You can then download images and store them in the Clip Art Gallery.

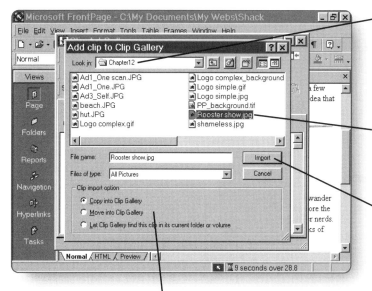

5. Navigate to the **directory** containing the image that you want to add to the Clip Art Gallery. The directory will appear in the Look in list box.

6. Click on the **image file** that you want to add. The image will be selected.

7. Click on **Import**. The Clip Properties dialog box will appear. The Description tab should be on top.

TIP

You can copy or move the image file to the Clip Art Gallery, or you can have the Gallery access it in its current location.

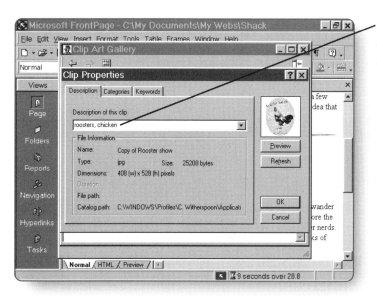

8. In the Description of this clip text box, **type** a **description** of the image you are adding to the Clip Art Gallery.

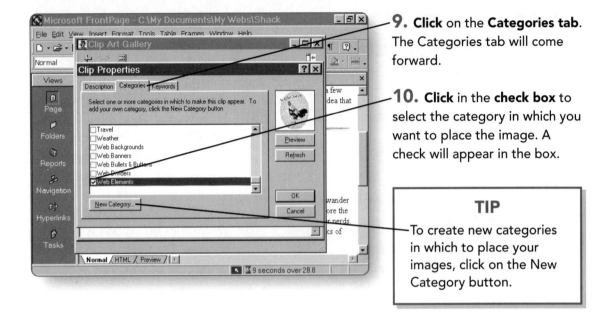

9. Click on the **Categories tab**. The Categories tab will come forward.

10. Click in the **check box** to select the category in which you want to place the image. A check will appear in the box.

TIP

To create new categories in which to place your images, click on the New Category button.

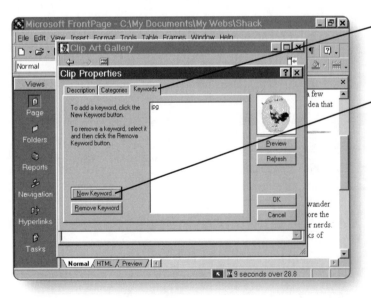

11. Click on the **Keywords tab**. The Keywords tab will come forward.

12. Click on the **New Keyword button**. The New Keyword dialog box will appear.

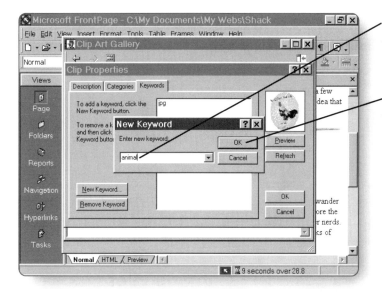

13. In the Enter new keyword text box, **type** a **keyword** that describes the image.

14. Click on **OK** to return to the Clip Properties dialog box.

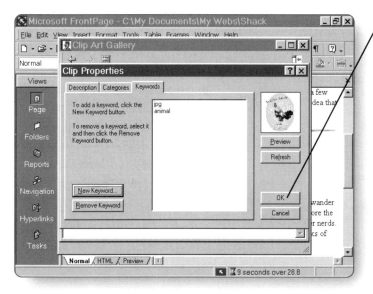

15. Click on **OK**. The Clip Art Gallery will appear showing the image in the selected category.

TIP

Click on the Preview button to display a larger image preview window.

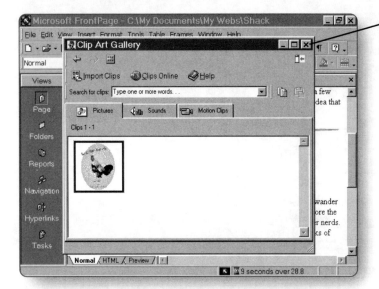

16. Click on the **Close button**. The Clip Art Gallery will close.

Using Your Own Image Files

If you want to dress up your Web page with an image stored on your computer, follow these simple steps.

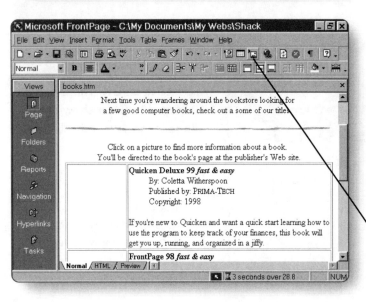

1. With your Web page open in the Page view, **click** on the **place** where you want to insert the image. The insertion bar will appear in the selected position.

2. Click on the **Insert Picture From File icon**. The Picture dialog box will open.

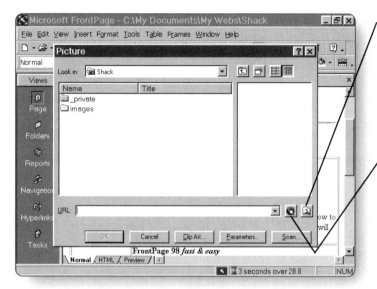

3. **Click** on the **Select a file on your computer button**. The Select File dialog box will open.

TIP

There are many places on the Internet where you can find free clip art for use in personal Web pages. People who post these images will also post any conditions for downloading and using them.

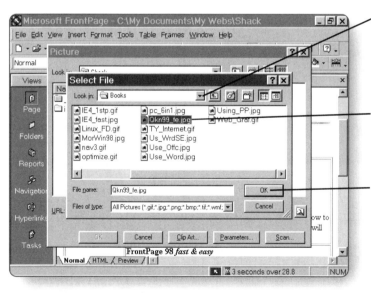

4. **Navigate** to the **folder** containing the image you want to use. The folder will appear in the Look in list box.

5. **Click** on the **image file** that you want to insert. The file will be selected.

6. **Click** on **OK**. The image will be inserted on the Web page.

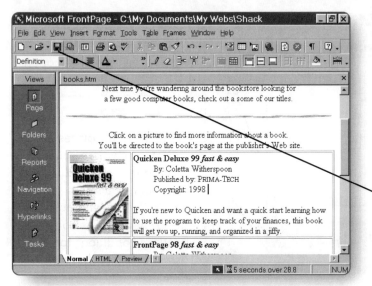

Saving Images to FrontPage

After you have added an image to a Web page, you will need to save the page. When you do this, FrontPage will ask you where you want to save the file.

1. Click on the **Save button**. The Save Embedded Files dialog box will appear.

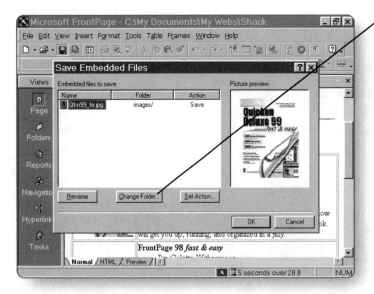

2. Click on the **Change Folder button**. The Change Folder dialog box will appear.

NOTE

You may want to store your images in their own folder, separate from your Web pages. By doing this, you will be able to find image files more easily. To learn more about managing files and folders, see Chapter 14, "Updating Your Web."

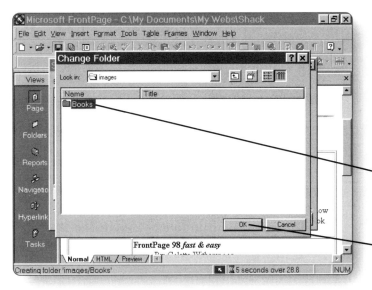

3. Click on the **folder** where
you want to save the image file.
The folder will be selected.

4. Click on **OK**. The Save
Embedded Files dialog box will
appear.

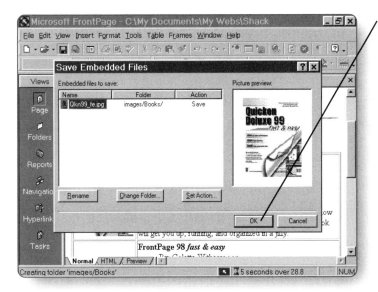

5. Click on **OK**. The image will
be saved to your Web site.

Wrapping Text around an Image

One of the new features of FrontPage allows you to wrap text around an image. You've probably seen this technique used most when placing a drop-cap in a paragraph.

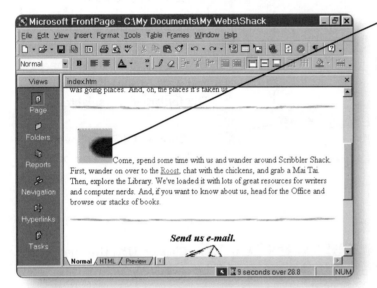

1. **Insert** the **picture** at the beginning of the paragraph that you want to wrap around the image. The bottom of the picture will be lined up with the bottom of the first line of text.

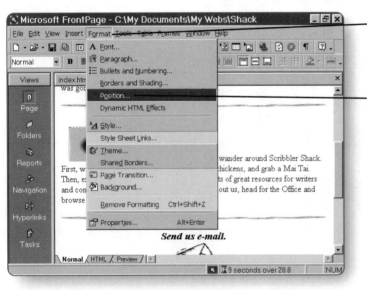

2. **Click** on **Format** on the menu bar. The Format menu will appear.

3. **Click** on **Position**. The Position dialog box will open.

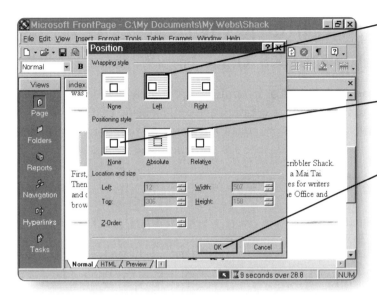

4. Click on the **Left icon** in the Wrapping style area. The icon will be selected.

5. Click on the **None icon** in the Positioning style area. The icon will be selected.

6. Click on **OK**.

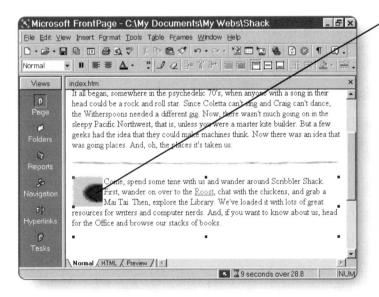

The top of the image will be even with the top of the first line of text, and the rest of the paragraph will flow around the image.

TIP

Go ahead and experiment with the other image positions.

Using Images for Hyperlinks on the Web

Images work well as hyperlinks. Creating a hyperlink using an image is as easy as creating a hyperlink using text. However, there are a few extra tricks you can learn to make your image hyperlinks more descriptive and appealing to your visitors.

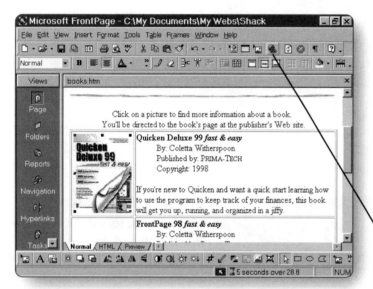

Creating an Image Hyperlink

1. With your Web page displayed in the Page view window, **click** on the **image** that you want to use as the hyperlink. The image will be selected.

2. Click on the **Hyperlink icon**. The Create Hyperlink dialog box will open.

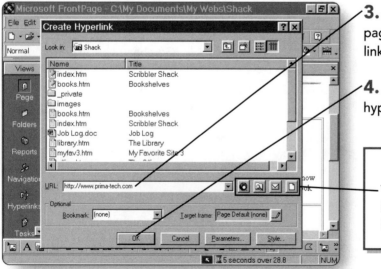

3. Type the **URL** of the Web page to which the image will link.

4. Click on **OK**. The image hyperlink will be created.

NOTE

You can also use the URL buttons to create the hyperlink.

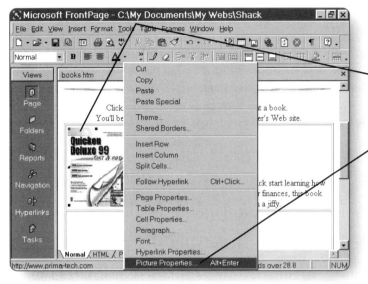

Creating a Border around an Image

1. Right-click on the **image** to which you want to apply a border. A menu will appear.

2. Click on **Picture Properties**. The Picture Properties dialog box will appear with the General tab at the front.

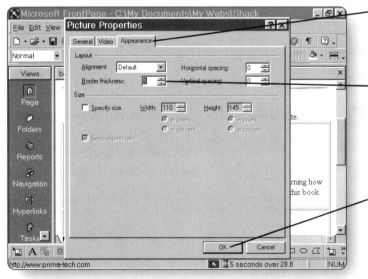

3. Click on the **Appearance tab**. The Appearance tab will come forward.

4. Click on the **up and down arrows** to select the border thickness for the image. The number in the text box will change.

5. Click on **OK**. A border will appear around the image. The thickness of the border will depend on your selection.

Using Low Resolution Images

If you have added an image to your Web page that has a large file size (and correspondingly, a long download time), you may want to add an alternate image. By using an alternate image with a smaller file size and lower resolution, visitors to your site will have something to look at while they are waiting for the larger image to download. After the larger image has downloaded, it will replace the lower resolution image.

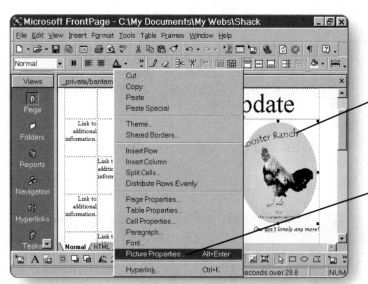

1. Right-click on the **image** that you want to use with an alternate picture. A menu will appear.

2. Click on **Picture Properties**. The Picture Properties dialog box will appear with the General tab at the front.

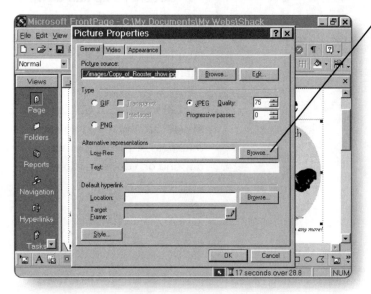

3. Click on the **Browse button** located in the Alternate representations section. The Select Alternate Picture dialog box will open.

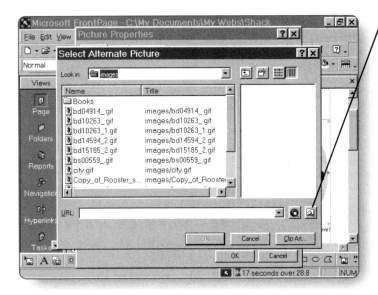

4. **Click** on the **Select a file on your computer button**. The Select File dialog box will open.

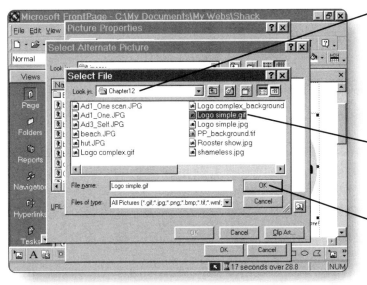

5. **Navigate** to the **drive and folder** where you've stored an image that you want to use as an alternate low-resolution image. The folder will appear in the Look in: list box.

6. **Select** a **low-resolution image**. The image file will be highlighted.

7. **Click** on **OK**. The Picture Properties box will return, and the path and file name for the image will appear in the Low-Res text box.

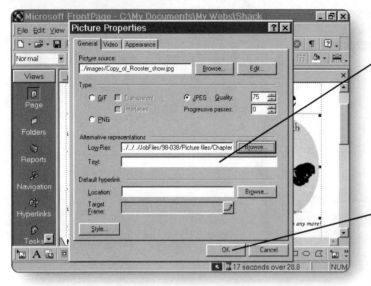

8. Click on **OK**. When a visitor accesses the page, the lower resolution image will appear first in the visitor's Web browser and will display until the higher-resolution image completely downloads.

Adding Background Images to Pages

If you used one of the FrontPage themes, your Web pages already have a background. If you aren't using a theme, you can still give your Web pages color and pizzazz with the right background image.

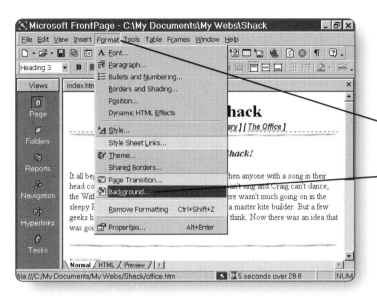

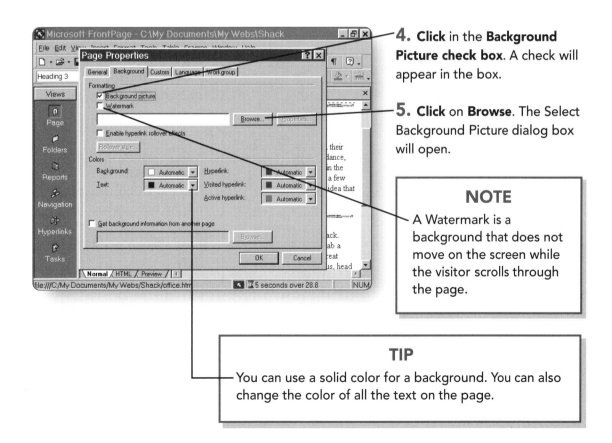

1. Open the **page** to which you want to add a background. The page will appear in the Page view window.

2. Click on **Format**. The Format menu will appear.

3. Click on **Background**. The Page Properties dialog box will open with the Background tab at the front.

4. Click in the **Background Picture check box**. A check will appear in the box.

5. Click on **Browse**. The Select Background Picture dialog box will open.

NOTE

A Watermark is a background that does not move on the screen while the visitor scrolls through the page.

TIP

You can use a solid color for a background. You can also change the color of all the text on the page.

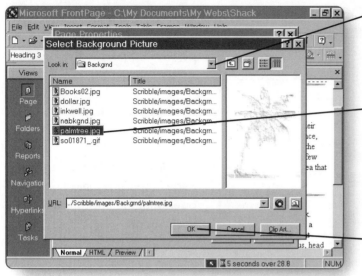

6. Navigate to the **folder** in which the background image is located. The folder will appear in the Look in list box.

7. Click on the **image file** that you want to use as the background. The image will be selected, and a preview of the image will appear on the right side of the dialog box.

8. Click on **OK**. The Page Properties dialog box will return showing the path and file name of the image.

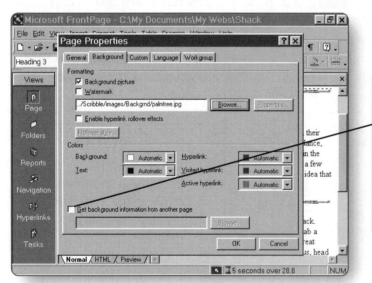

9. Click on **OK**. The background will be applied to the page.

TIP

To make a number of Web pages look similar, use the background and color information from a previously formatted page.

10

Working with Image Tools

After you've inserted a picture into a Web page, you may find that you want the picture to look different. Normally, you would open the picture in one of the many image-editing software programs and make your changes there. FrontPage contains a number of image-editing functions so that you don't have to use a second software program. You won't find all the bells and whistles, but you'll find some good basic tools that allow you to create a new look for your pictures. In this chapter, you'll learn how to:

- Edit image color
- Add edges and text to pictures
- Crop and rotate pictures
- Build an image map

Editing Images

The FrontPage image-editing tools are located on the Pictures toolbar. The Pictures toolbar appears above the Status Bar at the bottom of your screen whenever you select a picture. You can also display the Pictures toolbar by selecting it from the View, Toolbars menu.

Making Images Look Washed Out

The Wash Out command creates a light-colored (almost transparent) version of an image. This command is useful if you don't want an image to stand out on a page or if you want to place text over an image so that the text is readable.

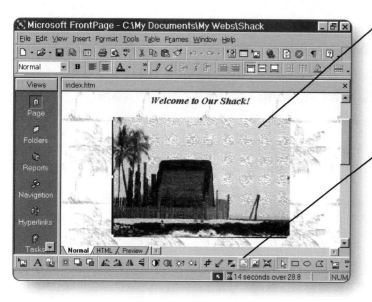

1. With your Web page displayed in the Page view window, **click** on the **image** to which you want to apply the washout effect. The image will be selected.

2. Click on the **Wash Out button** on the Pictures toolbar. The image will appear in paler colors.

TIP

If you don't like the effect, click on the Undo button on the Standard toolbar.

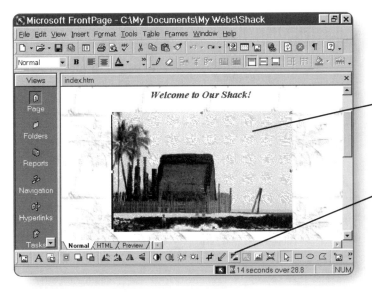

Turning Color Pictures Black and White

1. Click on the color **image** that you want to change to black and white. The image will be selected.

2. Click on the **Black and White button**. The image will look like a black and white photograph.

Changing the Contrast and Brightness of an Image

1. Click on the **image**. The image will be selected.

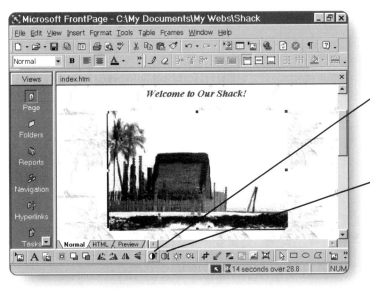

2. Click on the following **buttons** until the desired contrast and brightness are achieved:

● Select More Contrast to add more definition between the light and dark colors in the image.

● Select Less Contrast to soften images that are too harsh.

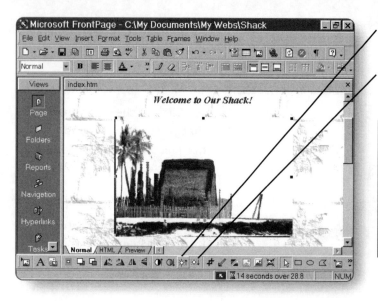

- Select More Brightness to lighten the image.

- Select Less Brightness to darken the image.

NOTE

The brightness and contrast buttons can be clicked more than once to achieve the desired effect in different degrees.

Adding Edges and Text

Words and frames can give your images a classy, finished look.

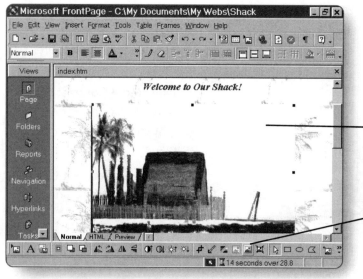

Adding a Beveled Edge to an Image

To place a frame effect around your images, follow these steps.

1. Click on the **image** to which you want to add a beveled edge. The image will be selected.

2. Click on the **Bevel button**. The beveled edge will be applied.

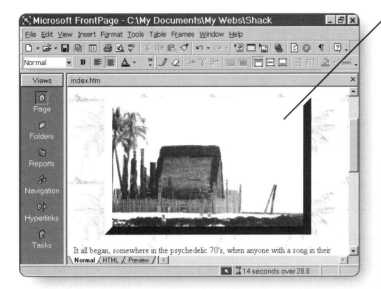

The image will appear to be framed. If you want to add more depth to the bevel edge, click on the Bevel button a few more times until you like the effect. Remember, you can always rely on the Undo button.

TIP

You can create a smaller image of the picture that will download faster to your visitor's Web browser by creating a thumbnail. When the visitor clicks on the thumbnail, they will be linked to a different page that displays the picture at its full size.

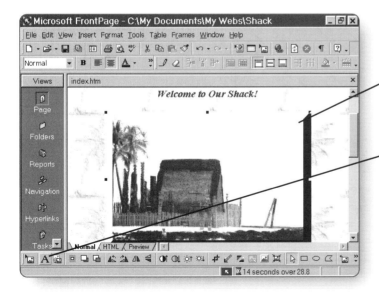

Placing Text Over an Image

1. Click on the **image** to which you want to add text. The image will be selected.

2. Click on the **Text button**. A text box will appear in the middle of the image, if the image is a GIF file. If the image is not a GIF file, FrontPage can automatically do this for you and will ask you for confirmation to proceed.

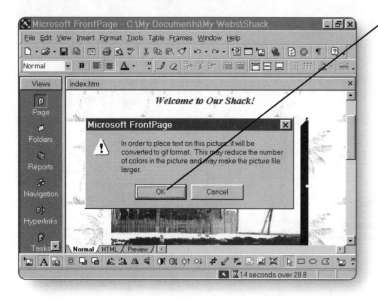

3. Click on **OK**. A text box will appear at the center of the image.

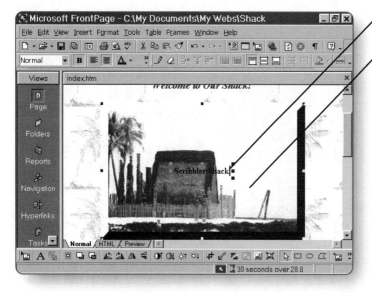

4. Type the **text**.

5. Click outside the text box when you are finished typing. The text will appear over the image.

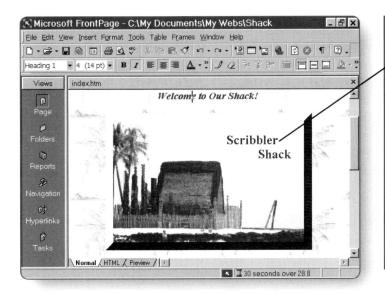

TIP

Text that is placed over images can be formatted in the same way as other text on your Web page. If you increase the size of the font, you'll need to make the text box larger. Click on a border handle and drag away from the text. Text boxes can also be moved to different positions on the image.

Changing Images More Dramatically

By cropping or rotating an image, you can change its visual effect on your Web page.

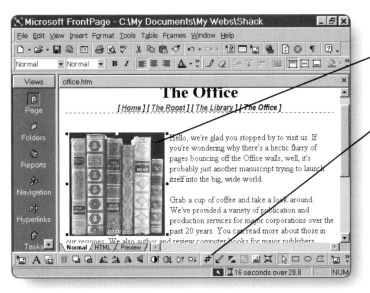

Cropping Images

1. Click on the **image** that you want to crop. The image will be selected.

2. Click on the **Crop button**. A blue box with image handles will appear around the image.

3. Place the **mouse pointer** over one of the image handles. The mouse pointer will turn into a double arrow.

4. Click and hold an **image handle**, then drag the mouse pointer toward the image. The crop marks will appear inside the image.

5. Release the **mouse button** when the undesired portion of the image is outside the crop marks.

6. Move the **crop marks** on the other sides of the image as needed.

7. Click on the **Crop button**. The cropped image will appear on the page.

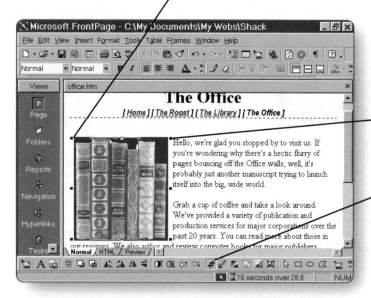

Only the desired portion of the image will remain on the Web page.

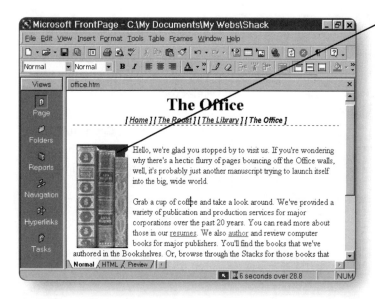

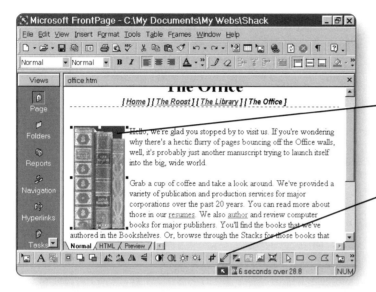

Making Image Backgrounds Transparent

1. **Click** on the **image** in which you want the background to disappear. The image will be selected.

2. **Click** on the **Set Transparent Color button**. The mouse pointer will turn into the eraser end of a pencil.

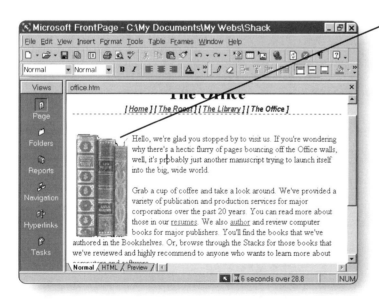

3. **Click** on the **background color** in the image. The image background will disappear, and the background of the Web page will appear in its place.

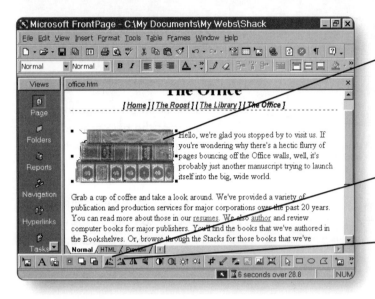

Rotating Images

1. Click on the **image**. The image will be selected.

2. Click on the following **icon buttons** until the desired position is achieved:

- **Rotate Left** to rotate the image counterclockwise by 90 degrees.

- **Rotate Right** to rotate the image clockwise by 90 degrees.

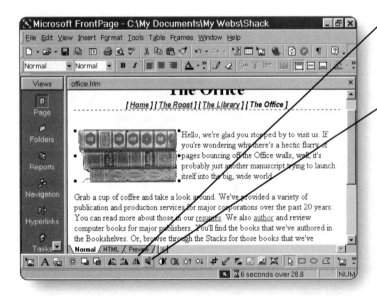

- **Flip Horizontal** turns the image around so that it appears you are looking at it from behind.

- **Flip Vertical** turns the image upside down.

NOTE

The rotation buttons can be clicked until the desired position is achieved.

Designing Image Maps

An image map is a single picture to which you will add a number of hyperlinks (in the form of hotspots). Image maps are an alternative way for visitors to navigate to the different pages in your Web site. An image map starts as a piece of artwork that you create from scanned photographs, computer drawings, or clip art. The artwork is created in a computer graphics program. You'll need to create this artwork using the GIF or JPEG format. The image is then inserted into a Web page, where you'll add hotspots to the image. These hotspots are hyperlinks to other pages within your Web.

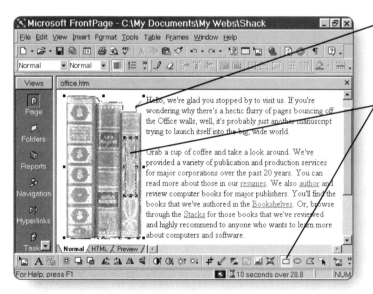

1. **Insert** the **image** that you want to use on the page.

2. **Choose** a **hotspot.**

- To create a hotspot over a rectangular shape, click on the Rectangular Hotspot button. Click on the upper-left corner of the area that you want to enclose in the hyperlink rectangle. Then drag the mouse to the lower-right corner of the desired section.

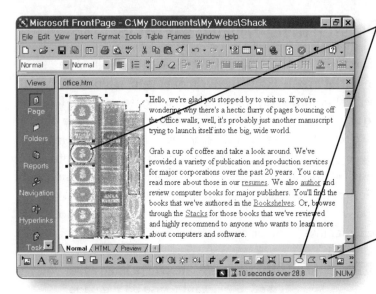

• To create a hotspot over a round shape, click on the Circular Hotspot button. Click in the image at the center of the area around which you want to draw the circle, and drag away from the center point.

TIP

If you want to check the placement of your hotspots, click on the Show Hotspots button. The image will disappear and you will see only the hotspot outlines. Click on the Show Hotspots button again to return to your image.

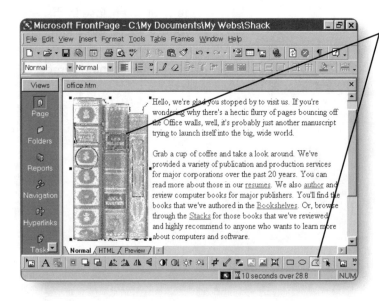

• To create a hotspot over an irregular shape, click on the Polygonal Hotspot button, click on the image at the first corner of the area, and click at each additional corner.

3. Release the **mouse button**. The Create Hyperlink dialog box will appear.

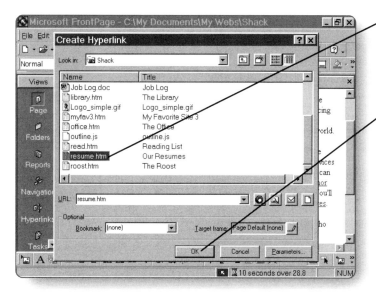

4. Click on the **page** to which you want to link. The file will be selected and will appear in the URL text box.

5. Click on **OK**. The hyperlink to the corresponding Web page will be created.

TIP

You can create a hotspot that links to a bookmark.

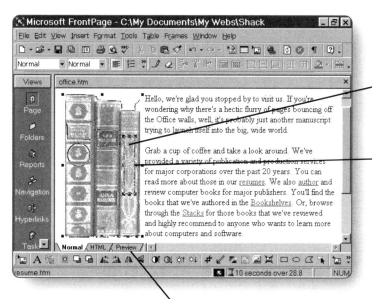

Changing the Size of a Hotspot

1. Click on the **hotspot** that you want to resize. The hotspot will be selected.

2. Place the **mouse pointer** over one of the image handles. The mouse pointer will turn into a double arrow.

TIP

You can see your image map in action. Click on the Preview tab. When you place the mouse over a hotspot, the name of the page to which it is linked will appear in the left end of the Status bar.

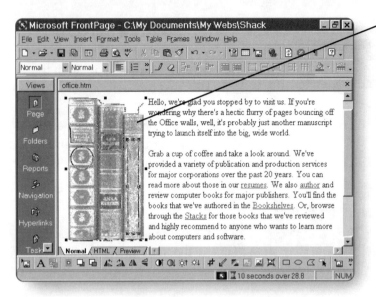

3. **Click and hold** the **mouse button** and **drag** the hotspot **outline** to the desired position.

4. **Release** the **mouse button**. The hotspot will be resized.

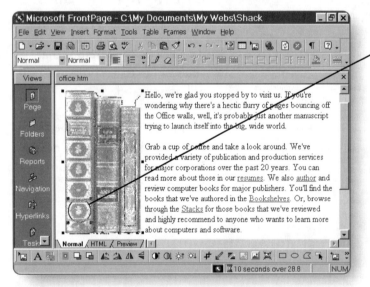

Moving Hotspots

1. **Click and hold** on the **hotspot** that you want to move. The hotspot will be selected. So that you don't accidentally resize the hotspot, be sure that the pointer is placed within the image handles, not on them.

2. **Drag** the **hotspot** to the new position and release the mouse button. The hotspot will be moved.

TIP

If you begin to move a hotspot and then decide you don't want it moved, press the Escape key.

11

Creating Dynamic Effects

Well-designed graphics can convey messages, but there may be times when you want your graphics to reach out and grab your audience. How can you convince your graphics to sing, dance, and perform? This has always been a relatively easy task for programmers. Now, even if you lack programming skills, you can make your graphics perform somersaults across the page using the built-in dynamic effects in FrontPage. In this chapter, you'll learn how to:

- Build flashy hover buttons
- Create banners that display like a slide show
- Make your messages move with marquees
- Use Dynamic HTML on your pages

Using Hover Buttons

You may have noticed that some Web pages contain graphics that change their appearance when you place the mouse pointer over them. These graphics are called hover buttons.

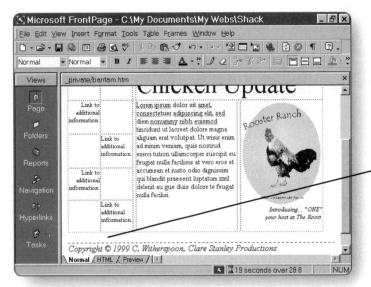

Creating Standard Hover Buttons

1. **Open** the **page** where you want the hover button to appear. The page will display in the Page view window.

2. **Click** on the **place** where you want to position the hover button. The insertion bar will appear in the selected location.

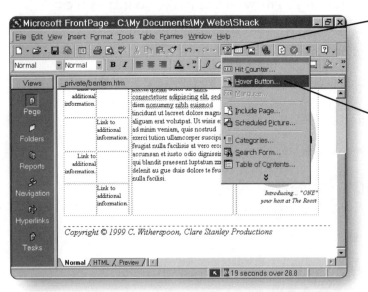

3. **Click** on the **Insert Component button** on the Standard toolbar. The Insert Component menu will appear.

4. **Click** on **Hover Button**. The Hover Button Properties dialog box will open and you'll see the beginning of a hover button on the Web page.

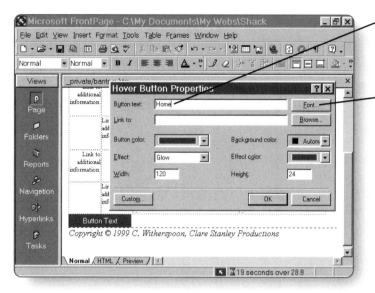

5. Type the **text** that will appear on the hover button in the Button text: text box.

6. Click on the **Font button**. The Font dialog box will open.

7. Click on the **down arrow** next to the Font drop-down list and **select** a **font** to be used on the hover button. The font name will display in the list box.

8. Click on the **down arrow** next to the Font Style drop-down list and **select** a **font style** for the hover button. The font style name will appear in the list box.

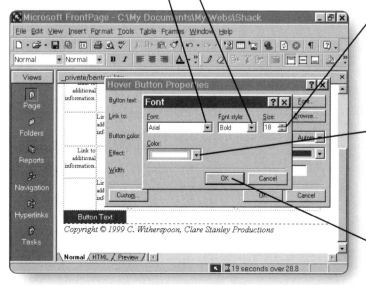

9. Click on the **up and down arrows** next to the Size list box and **select** a **font size** for the hover button. The font size will appear in the box.

10. Click on the **down arrow** next to the Color drop-down list box and **select** a **font color** for the hover button. The font color will show in the list box.

11. Click on **OK**. The Hover Button Properties dialog box will return.

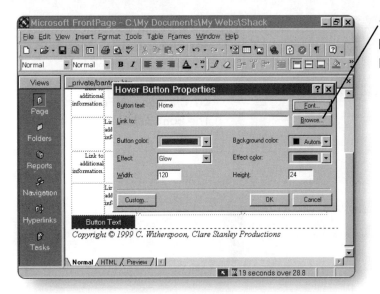

12. Click on the **Browse button**. The Select Hover Button Hyperlink dialog box will open.

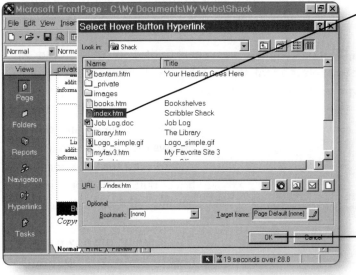

13. Locate the **folder** containing the page to which you want to create a hyperlink. **Click** on the **file name** for the page.

NOTE

For help creating a hyperlink, see Chapter 6, "Working with Hyperlinks."

14. Click on **OK**. The Hover Button Properties dialog box will open.

15. **Click** on the **down arrow** next to the Button color list box and **select** a **color** to be used in the foreground of the hover button. The color will appear in the list box.

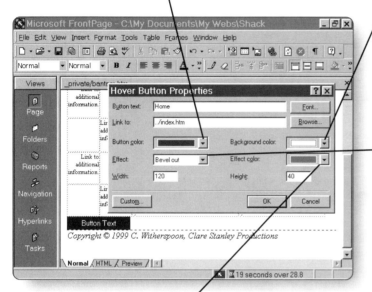

16. **Click** on the **down arrow** next to the Background color list box and **select** a **color** for the background of the hover button. The color will appear in the list box.

17. **Click** on the **down arrow** next to the Effect list box and **select** an **effect** that will appear when your visitors place the mouse pointer over the hover button. The effect name will appear in the list box.

18. **Click** on the **down arrow** next to the Effect color list box and **select** a **color** for the effect. The effect color will display in the list box.

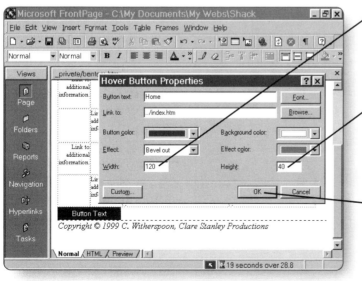

19. **Double-click** in the **Width text box** and **type** the desired **width** of the hover button, in pixels.

20. **Double-click** in the **Height text box** and **type** the desired **height** of the hover button, in pixels.

21. **Click** on **OK**. The hover button will be created.

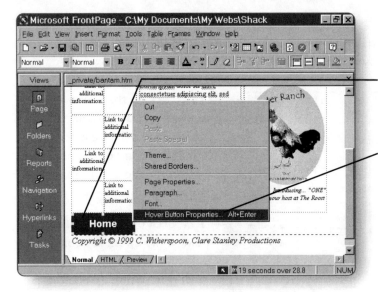

Editing Hover Buttons

1. Right-click on the **hover button** that you want to change. A shortcut menu will appear.

2. Click on **Hover Button Properties**. The Hover Button Properties dialog box will open.

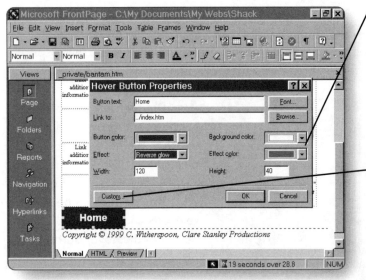

3. Make the **changes** to the hover button.

4. Click on **OK** to apply the changes.

TIP

To be creative, click on the Custom button. The resulting dialog box allows you to play a sound when the hover button is clicked. It also lets you use your own images as hover buttons.

Creating Banners

The Banner Ad Manager lets you take several images and display them in a slideshow fashion. The pictures flip from one to the next at set intervals. You can also add transition effects between images for even more pizzazz.

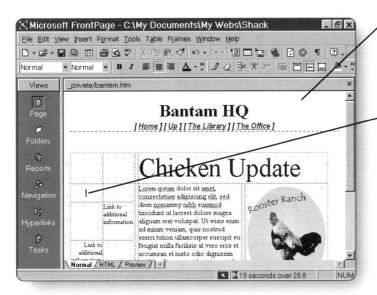

1. **Open** the **page** where you want to place the banner. The page will appear in the Page view window.

2. **Click** on the **place** where you want to position the banner. The insertion bar will appear in the selected location.

3. **Click** on the **Insert Component button**. The Insert Component menu will appear.

4. **Click** on **Banner Ad Manager**. The Banner Ad Manager Properties dialog box will open.

5. **Double-click** in the **Width text box** and **type** the **number** of pixels wide you want the banner to be.

6. **Double-click** in the **Height text box** and **type** the **number** of pixels high you want to banner to be.

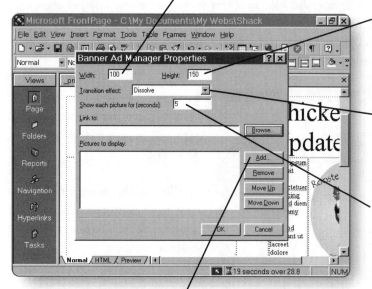

7. **Click** on the **down arrow** to the right of the Transition effect list box and **select** an **effect** for the transition between images.

8. **Double-click** in the **Show each image for (seconds) text box** and **type** the **number** of seconds to display each image.

9. **Click** on the **Add button** to add the first image in the banner. The Add Picture for Banner Ad dialog box will open.

NOTE

You can hyperlink the banner to another Web page by typing the URL of the page in the Link to text box. You can also click on the Browse button to locate the Web page.

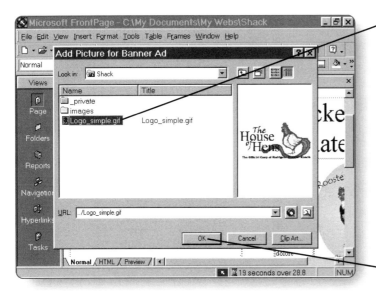

10. Select the **image** that you want to place in the banner. The path and file name of the image will appear in the URL text box.

11. Click on **OK**. The image file will be added to the Pictures to Display list in the Banner Ad Manager properties dialog box.

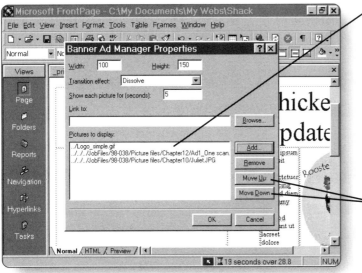

12. Repeat steps **9 through 11** to add any additional images. The image files will be added to the Pictures to Display list.

13. Click on **OK**. The banner will appear on the page.

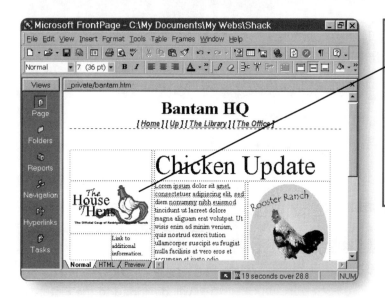

TIP

If you want to change the appearance of the banner, right-click on the banner and select Banner Ad Manager Properties. To see your banner in action, you will need to preview it in a Web browser.

Adding a Marquee

Marquees are a great way to get your visitor's attention because they move text across the Web page. If you add a marquee to a Web page, visitors to your Web site that are using Netscape Navigator will not be able to see this marquee.

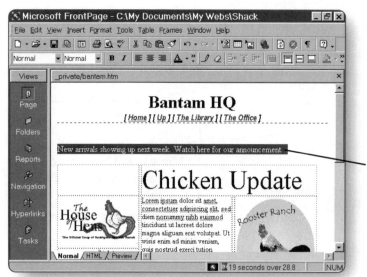

1. Open the **page** where you want to place the marquee. The page will display in the Page view window.

2. Type the **text** that you want to display in the marquee.

3. Select the **text** you just typed. The text will be highlighted.

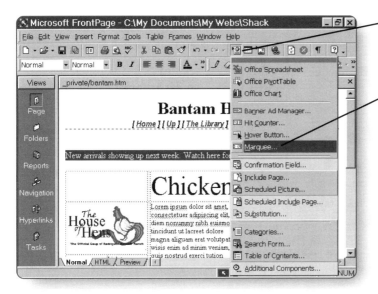

4. Click on the **Insert Component button**. The Insert Component menu will appear.

5. Click on **Marquee**. The Marquee Properties dialog box will open with the selected text in the Text text box.

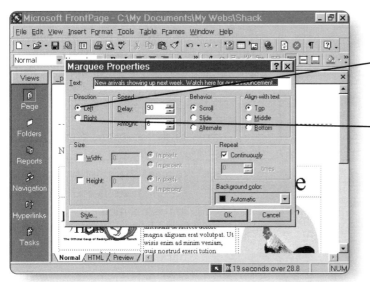

6. Click on a **Direction option button**:

- **Left** moves the marquee from the right side of the screen toward the left side.

- **Right** moves the marquee from the left side of the screen toward the right side.

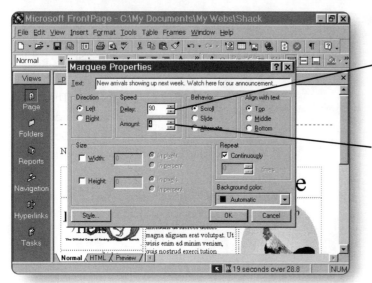

7. **Click** on the **Speed up** and **down arrows**:

- **Delay** sets the number of milliseconds before the marquee begins to move the text across the screen.

- **Amount** sets the increment, measured in pixels, by which the text will advance as it moves across the screen.

8. **Click** on a **Behavior option button**:

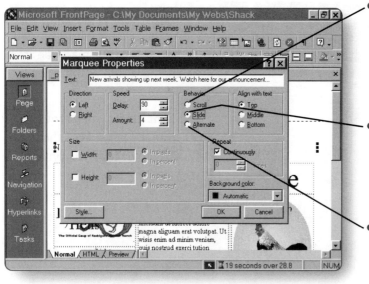

- **Scroll** brings the text in on one side of the screen and moves it toward the other side, where it disappears and then reappears at its original entry point.

- **Slide** moves the text in from one side, and when the text reaches the other side of the screen, it stops and remains in this position.

- **Alternate** moves the text back and forth across the screen.

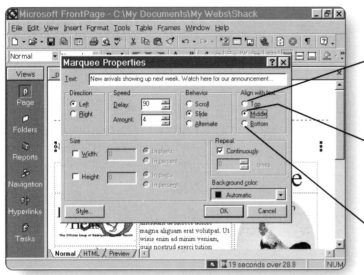

9. Click on an **Align with Text option button**:

- **Top** aligns the top of the marquee text with the top of any text that may appear on the same line.

- **Middle** aligns the middle of the marquee text with the middle of any text on the same line.

- **Bottom** aligns the bottom of the marquee text with the bottom of any text on the same line.

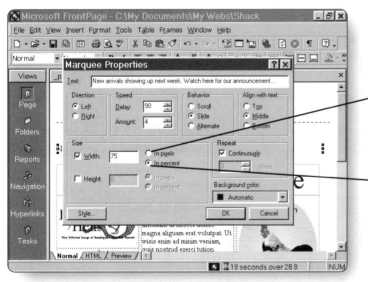

10. Set the **Size** of the marquee, if you want the marquee border to extend beyond the marquee text:

- The **In pixels** option button allows you to set an exact, fixed height or width for the marquee.

- The **In percent** option button causes the marquee to appear in different sizes on different screens, depending on the screen size and screen resolution.

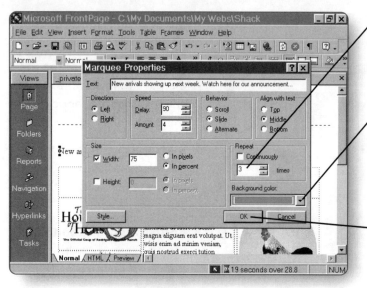

11. In the Repeat section, **select** the **number** of repetitions you want the marquee to move across the screen.

12. Click on the **down arrow** next to the Background Color list box and **select** a **color** that will appear behind the marquee text.

13. Click on **OK**. The marquee will appear on the page.

Adding Dynamic HTML Effects

Dynamic HTML is the newest addition to FrontPage that adds motion to your pages.

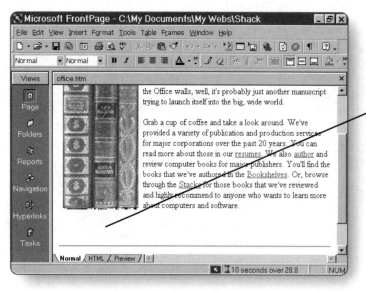

1. Open the **page** on which you want to add dynamic effects. The page will display in the Page view window.

2. Click in the **place** where you want to put the dynamic effect. The insertion bar will appear in the selected position.

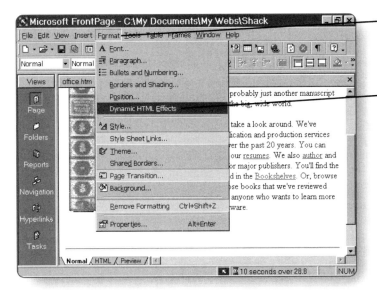

3. Click on **Format** on the menu bar. The Format menu will appear.

4. Click on **Dynamic HTML Effects**. The DHTML Effects toolbar will appear.

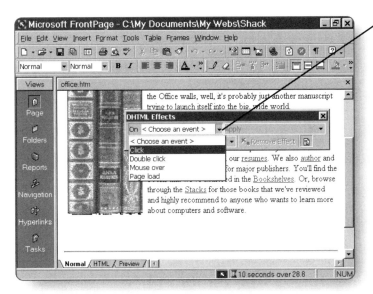

5. Click on the **down arrow** next to the On list box and select the event that will trigger the dynamic effect. The event name will display in the list box.

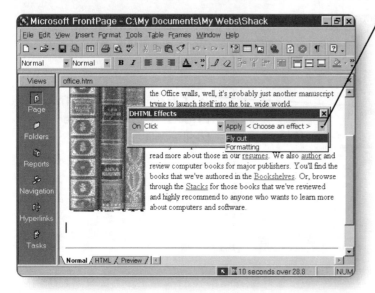

6. Click on the **down arrow** next to the first Apply list box and select the effect that should result when the event occurs. The effect name will display in the list box.

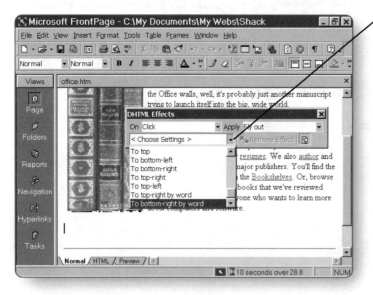

7. Click on the **down arrow** next to the second Apply list box and select the setting that controls the effect's motion in the browser window. The setting name will show in the list box, and an Effect box will appear on the Web page.

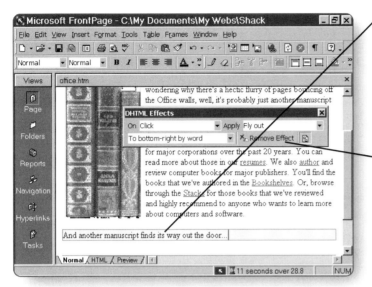

8. **Click** in the **Effect box** on the page, and **type** the **text** that you want to include in the dynamic effect.

TIP

If you no longer want to use the dynamic effect on the Web page, click on the Remove Effect button.

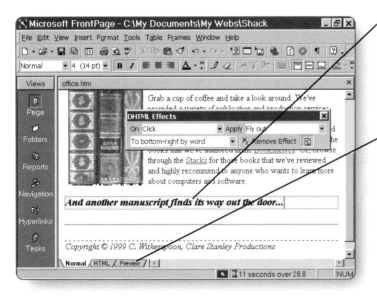

9. **Select** the **text** and **use** the **text formatting tools** to change the appearance of the text. You can change the size, style, and color of the selected text.

10. **Click** on the **Preview tab** or the **Preview in Browser button**. Your default Web browser will open so that you can see the dynamic effect in action.

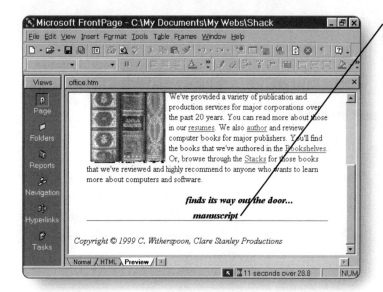

You'll see the text float down the page and drop into place.

12

Working with Forms

The easiest way to collect information, sell products, or conduct surveys on the Web is by using forms. Forms on the Web resemble the paper forms that you fill out all the time. The folks at Microsoft have developed a way for you to create a form that will automatically be functional when you publish it to your Web site. In this chapter, you'll learn how to:

- Get a quick and easy start on your form
- Collect responses from your form page
- Edit your form by adding additional form fields
- Include boxes and buttons on the form
- Allow users to select responses from drop-down lists

Creating the Form

The easiest way to build your form is to use the Form Page Wizard. The wizard walks you through the steps needed to create the form and suggests question topics for your visitors. The wizard generates the form and includes a way for your visitors to send their responses to you.

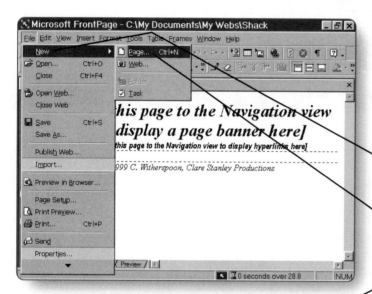

1. Open a blank **page**. The blank Page view window will appear.

2. Click on **File** on the menu bar. The File menu will appear.

3. Click on **New**. A second menu will appear.

4. Click on **Page**. The New dialog box will open with the General tab on top.

5. Click on **Form Page Wizard**. The wizard will be selected.

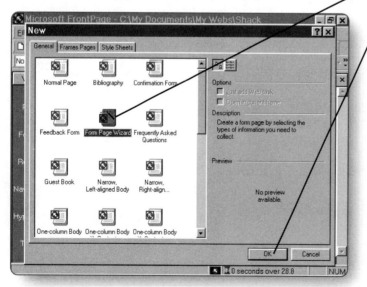

6. Click on **OK**. The Form Page Wizard will begin.

TIP

In addition to using the Form Page Wizard, you can start your form by selecting the Confirmation Form, Feedback Form, Guest Book, or User Registration template from the New dialog box.

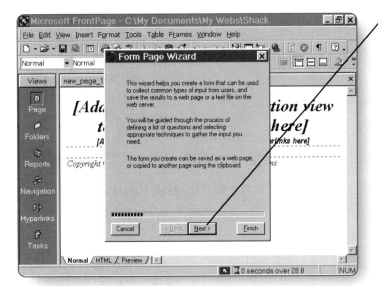

7. **Click** on **Next**. The next page of the wizard will appear.

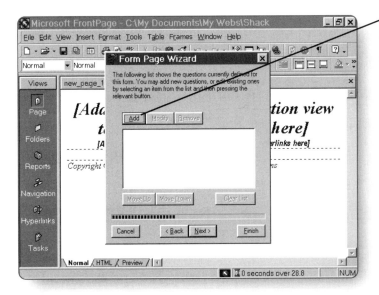

8. **Click** on the **Add button**. The next page of the wizard will allow you to choose from a variety of predefined form questions.

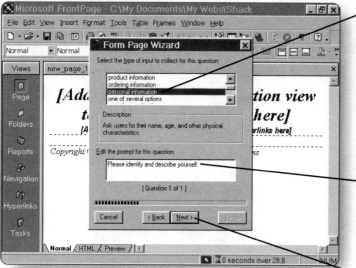

9. Click on a form **question** in the Select the type of input to collect for this question list. A description of the question will display in the Description box, and a sample leading question will appear in the Edit the prompt for this question text box.

10. Make any **changes** to the question that appears in the Edit the prompt for this question text box.

11. Click on **Next**. A screen asking for the type of information to collect will appear.

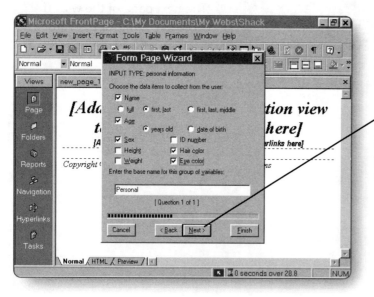

12. Put a **check mark** in the boxes associated with the information that you want to collect.

13. Click on **Next**. The next page of the wizard will appear showing the type of input that will be collected on the form.

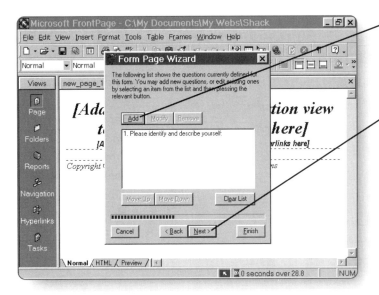

14. **Repeat steps 8 through 13** until all the information that you want collected on the form appears in the list.

15. **Click** on **Next**. The next page of the wizard will appear.

16. **Click** on an **option** from the How should the list of questions be presented? section. The option will be selected.

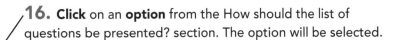

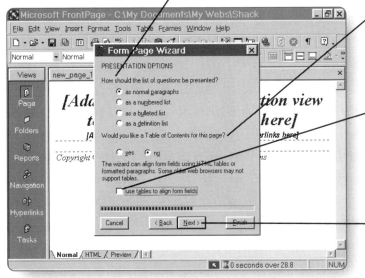

17. **Click** on an **option** from the Would you like a Table of Contents for this page? section. The option will be selected.

18. If you want to determine how your form will be formatted, **put** a **check mark** in the use tables to align form fields check box.

19. **Click** on **Next**. The next page of the wizard will appear.

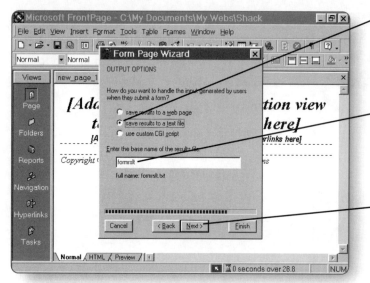

20. **Click** on an **option button** to select how you want the results of the form to be saved. The option will be selected.

21. In the Enter the base name of the results file text box, **type** a **file name** for the file in which the results will be collected.

22. **Click** on **Next**. The last page of the wizard will appear.

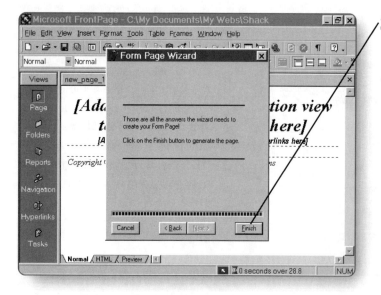

23. **Click** on **Finish**.

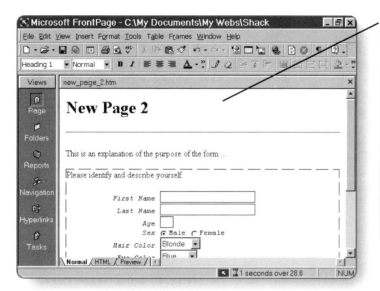

You will see your form in the Page view window.

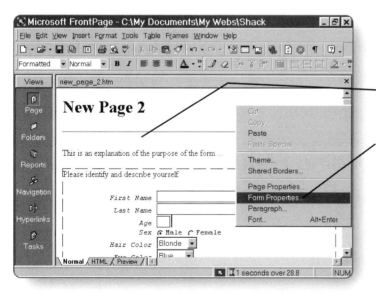

Handling Responses

1. Right-click on the **form**. A shortcut menu will appear.

2. Click on **Form Properties**. The Form Properties dialog box will open.

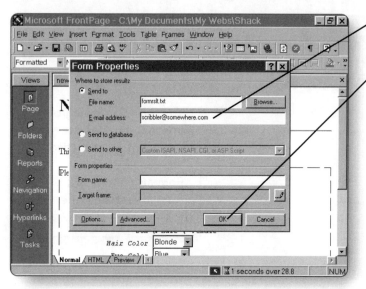

3. **Type** your **e-mail address** in the E-mail Address text box.

4. **Click** on **OK**. When a visitor to your site submits the form, the responses will be sent to you as an e-mail message.

TIP

If your ISP does not support the FrontPage Server Extensions, you cannot have replies sent to your e-mail address. Form results can be saved as a file on your ISP's server along with your Web pages. You'll need to use an FTP program to access your Web space and download the file to your computer.

Adding Fields to the Form Page

After you have used the Form Page Wizard to create a form, you can go back and add new fields to the form.

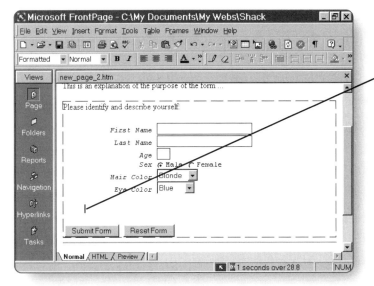

Creating a One-Line Text Box

1. Click at the end of the **line** preceding the space where you want to add the new form field. The insertion bar will appear at the end of the line.

2. Press Enter. A new line will appear.

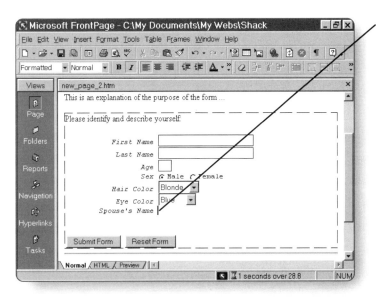

3. Type the **text** that you want to ask or tell your visitor. If you want to place the form field on the line below the text, **press Enter**.

NOTE

You can format your questions as bullet points to make them stand out. Try using an image bullet.

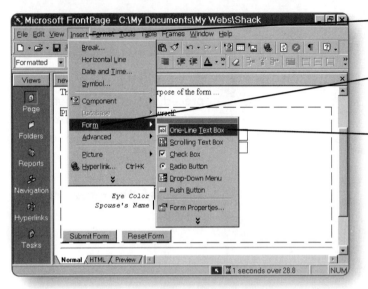

4. **Click** on **Insert** on the menu bar. The Insert menu will appear.

5. **Click** on **Form**. A second menu will appear.

6. **Click** on **One-Line Text Box**. A one-line form field will appear on the page.

NOTE

You can turn the Form drop-down menu into a toolbar. Click and hold the bar at the top of the menu and drag it away from the Insert menu. You can place this toolbar in any position on your screen.

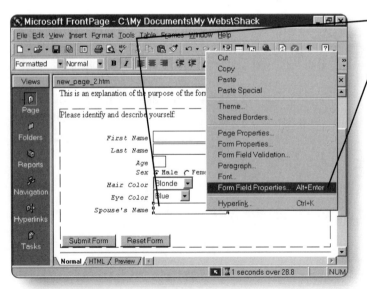

7. **Right-click** on the **text box**. A shortcut menu will appear.

8. **Click** on **Form Field Properties**. The Text Box Properties dialog box will open.

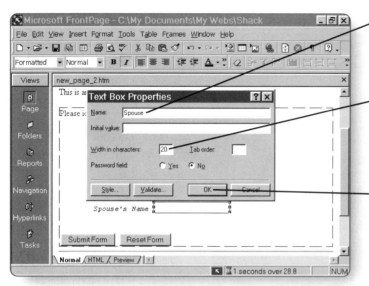

9. Type a descriptive **name** for the information that will be collected in the text box.

10. Type the **number** of characters you want the text box to display in the Width in characters text box.

11. Click on **OK**. The text box will be resized.

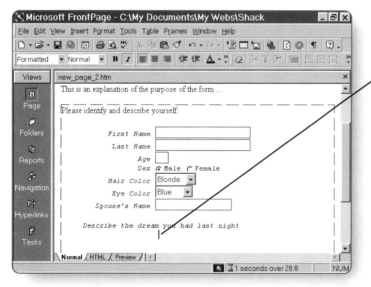

Using Scrolling Boxes

1. Click in the **place** where you want to add a scrolling text box. The insertion bar will appear.

2. Type the **text** that you want to use as a lead-in to the form field and **press Enter**.

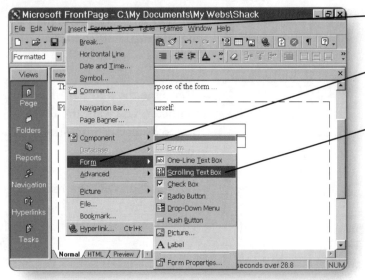

3. Click on **Insert**. The Insert menu will appear.

4. Click on **Form**. A second menu will appear.

5. Click on **Scrolling Text Box**. A text box with scroll bars will appear on the page.

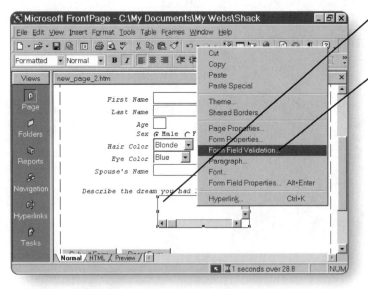

6. Right-click on the **scroll box**. A shortcut menu will appear.

7. Click on **Form Field Validation**. The Text Box Validation dialog box will appear.

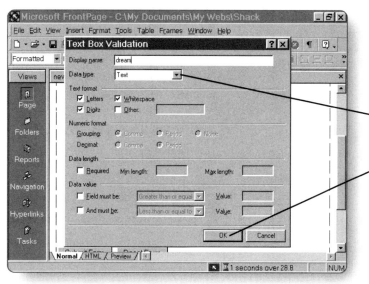

8. Click on the **down arrow** next to the Data Type drop-down list. A list of options will appear.

9. Click on a **data type**. The option will be selected.

10. Click on **OK**. Visitors to your site will only be able to enter the type of data you specified into the scroll box.

Including Boxes and Buttons

Check boxes and option buttons allow visitors to your form page to select from a variety of options. These boxes and buttons are easy to create.

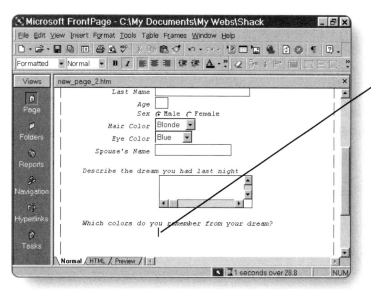

Creating Check Boxes

1. Click in the **place** where you want to add the check boxes. The insertion bar will appear on the page in the selected place.

2. Type the **text** that you want to use as a lead-in to the form field and **press Enter**.

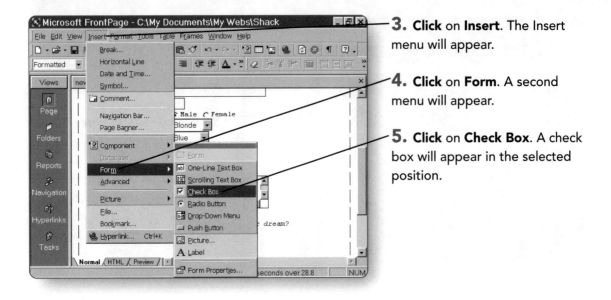

3. Click on **Insert**. The Insert menu will appear.

4. Click on **Form**. A second menu will appear.

5. Click on **Check Box**. A check box will appear in the selected position.

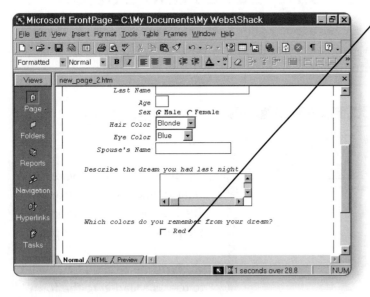

6. Type text to describe the purpose of the text box and **press Enter**.

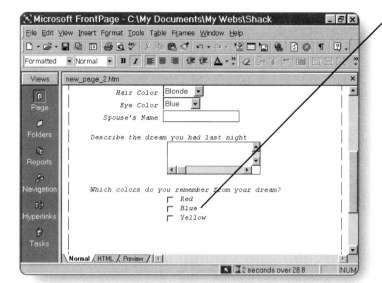

7. **Add** additional **check boxes** to complete the response options to the question.

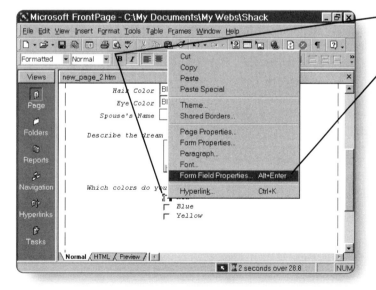

8. **Right-click** on a **check box**. A shortcut menu will appear.

9. **Click** on **Form Field Properties**. The Check Box Properties dialog box will open.

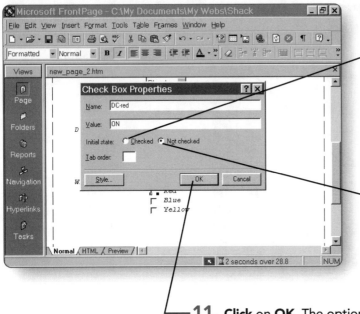

10. Choose one of the **options** from the Initial State section:

- **Checked**. Automatically places a check mark in the check box so that your visitor does not need to do this. Your visitors will still be able to clear this check box if they want.

- **Not Checked**. Leaves the check box blank, giving your visitor the option to leave the box unchecked or to check the box.

11. Click on **OK**. The option will be applied to the check box.

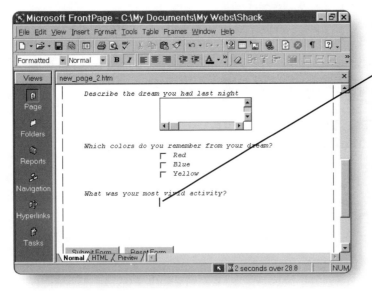

Adding Option Buttons

1. Click in the **place** where you want to add the option button. The insertion bar will appear.

2. Type the **text** that you want to use as a lead-in to the form field and **press Enter**.

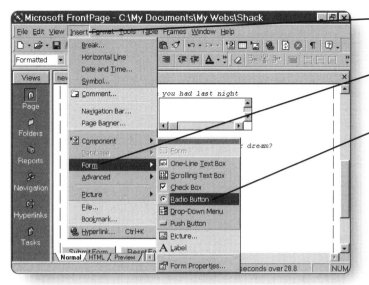

3. Click on **Insert**. The Insert menu will appear.

4. Click on **Form**. A second menu will appear.

5. Click on **Radio Button**. An option button will appear in the selected position.

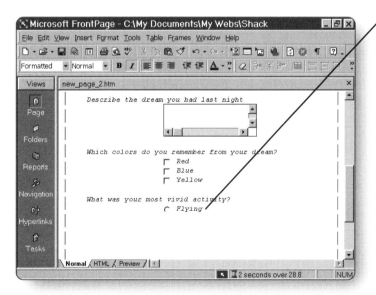

6. Type text to describe the purpose of the option button and **press Enter**.

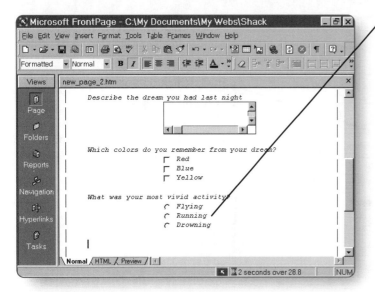

7. **Add** additional **option buttons** to complete the response options to the question.

Creating Drop-Down Lists

Drop-down lists allow you to give your visitors a number of options from which to choose. They also take up less space on the form than check boxes or option buttons.

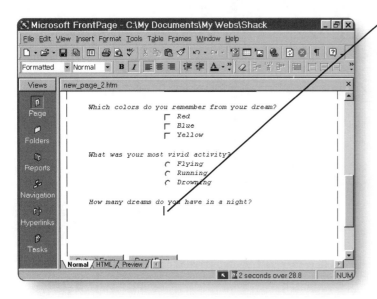

1. **Click** in the **place** where you want to add the drop-down list. The insertion bar will appear.

2. **Type** the **text** that you want to use as a lead-in to the form field and **press Enter**.

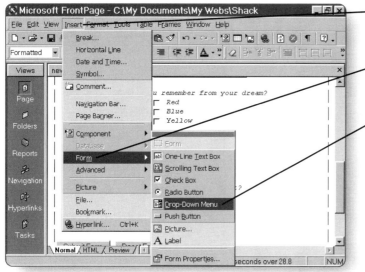

3. Click on **Insert**. The Insert menu will appear.

4. Click on **Form**. A second menu will appear.

5. Click on **Drop-Down Menu**. A drop-down list will appear in the selected position.

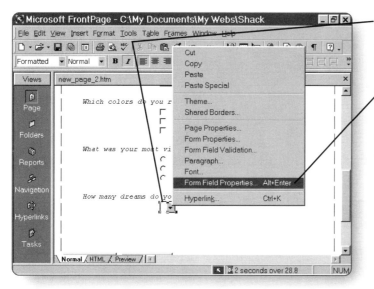

6. Right-click on the **drop-down list**. A shortcut menu will appear.

7. Click on **Form Field Properties**. The Drop-Down Menu Properties dialog box will open.

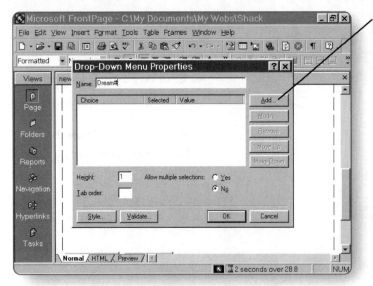

8. **Click** on the **Add button**. The Add Choice dialog box will appear.

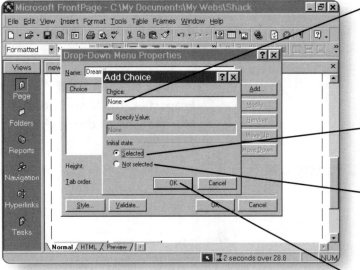

9. In the Choice text box, **type** the **text** that you want to include in the drop-down list.

10. **Choose** one of the **options** in the Initial State section:

- **Selected**. This text will appear initially in the text box that displays the drop-down list.

- **Not Selected**. This text will be hidden until the visitor clicks on the down arrow next to the drop-down list.

11. **Click** on **OK**. The text will be added to the Drop-Down Menu Properties dialog box.

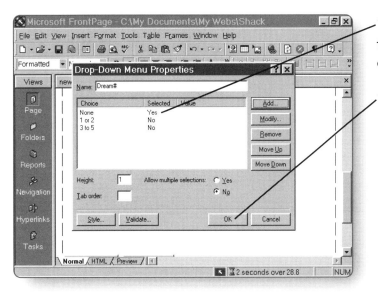

12. Add additional **choices** that you want to offer in the drop-down list.

13. Click on **OK**.

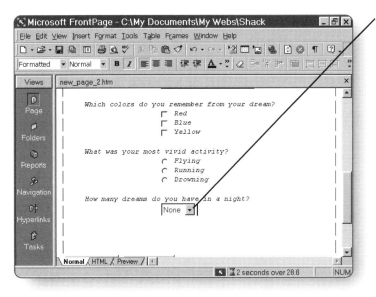

The drop-down list will be created.

13

Working with Frames

You've learned about two methods that enable your visitors to move smoothly from page to page: hyperlinks and navigation buttons. You can also offer easy navigation by using frames. Frames divide the Web browser window into several separate areas, each of which contains its own Web page. The most common arrangement of frames is a double layout in which one frame provides the navigation element of the page and the other displays Web page content. When a visitor to your site clicks on a link in the navigation frame, the corresponding page appears in the other frame. In this chapter, you'll learn how to:

- Build a basic frames page
- Modify the look and feel of the frames page
- Add and delete frames from the frames page

Creating the Frames Page

A standard frames setup consists of the navigation frame and the Web pages that will be linked to the content frame. Before you begin creating your frames page, you should create the Web pages that will be linked to it. It's possible to create the pages while you are building the frames page, but it is much easier to have these pages done in advance. This section will show you how to create a simple frames page.

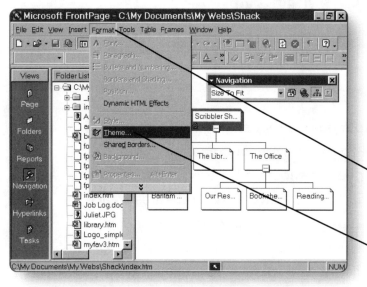

Preparing Your Web Pages for the Frames Page

1. **Open** the **Web** or **page** that you want to use in the frames page.

2. **Click** on **Format** on the menu bar. The Format menu will appear.

3. **Click** on **Theme**. The Choose Theme dialog box will open.

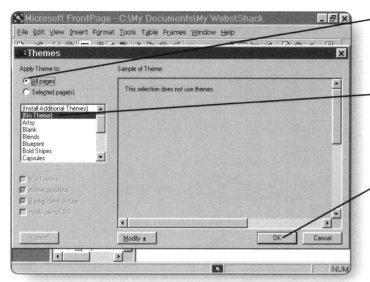

4. Click on the **All Pages option button**. The option will be selected.

5. Click on the **No Theme option** from the Apply Theme to list. The option will be selected.

6. Click on **OK**. Any theme elements that may have been applied to the pages in your Web will be removed.

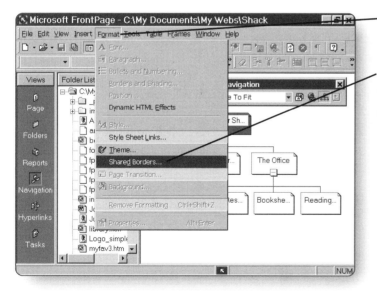

7. Click on **Format**. The Format menu will appear.

8. Click on **Shared Borders**. The Shared Borders dialog box will open.

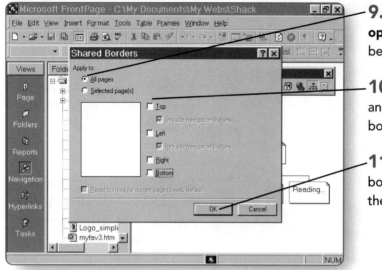

9. Click on the **All Pages option button**. The option will be selected.

10. **Clear** the Top, Left, Right, and Bottom **check boxes**. The boxes will be blank.

11. **Click** on **OK**. The shared borders will be removed from all the pages in the Web.

Building the Basic Frames Page

1. **Open** the **page** that you want to use as the home page of your frames-based Web site. The page will appear in the Page view window.

2. **Click** on **File**. The File menu will appear.

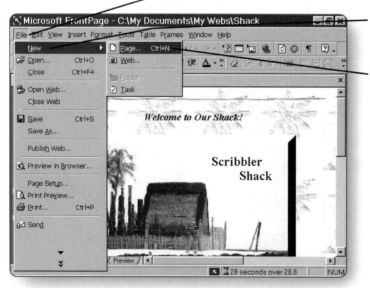

3. **Click** on **New**. A second menu will appear.

4. **Click** on **Page**. The New dialog box will open.

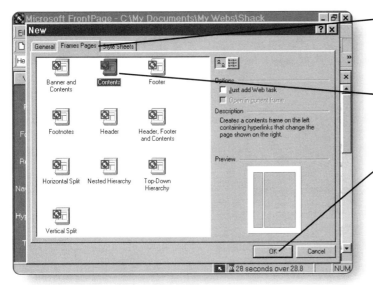

5. Click on the **Frames Pages tab**. The Frames Pages tab will come forward.

6. Click on the **style** of frame that you want to build. The template will be selected.

7. Click on **OK**. The frame template will appear.

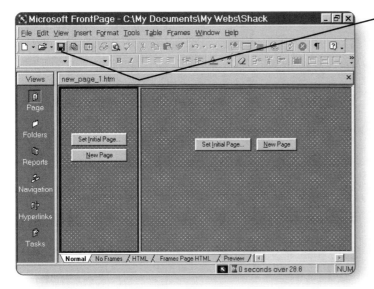

8. Click on the **Save button**. The Save As dialog box will appear with the frame set highlighted in the preview pane.

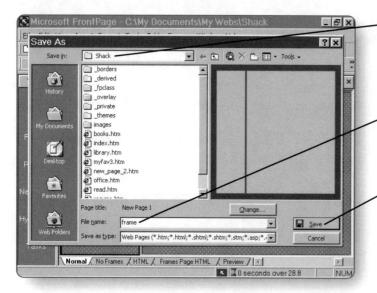

9. Click on the **folder** in which you want to save the frames page. The folder will be selected.

10. Type a **file name** for the frames page in the File name text box.

11. Click on **Save**. The frames page will be saved.

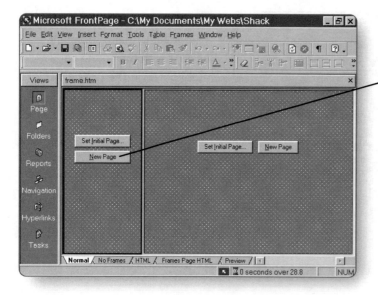

Filling the Frames with Web Pages

1. Click on the **New Page button** in the navigation frame. A blank page will appear in the frame area.

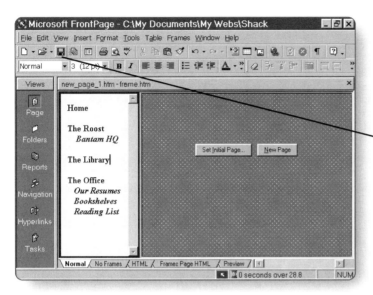

2. Create the navigation **content** that you want to appear in the frame when the page appears in your visitor's Web browser.

3. Click on the **Save button**. The Save As dialog box will appear with the frame highlighted in the preview pane.

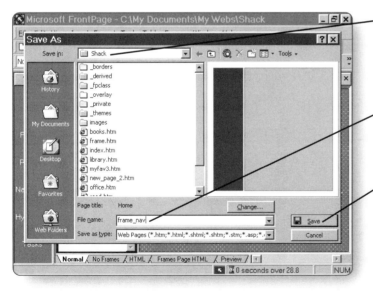

4. Click on the **folder** where you want to save the frames page. The folder will be selected.

5. Type a **file name** for this portion of the frames page in the URL text box.

6. Click on **Save**. The frame will be saved.

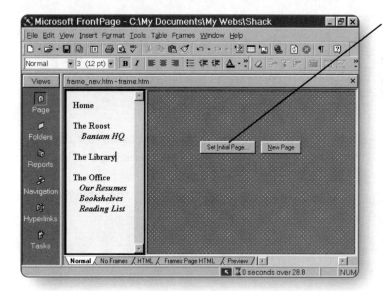

7. **Click** on the **Set Initial Page button** in the content frame. The Create Hyperlink dialog box will open.

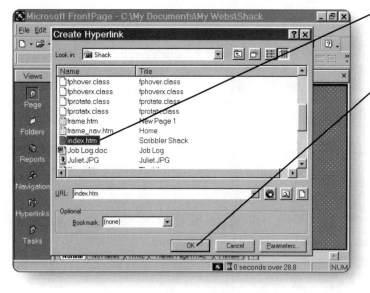

8. **Click** on the first **page** that you want your visitor to see. The page will be selected.

9. **Click** on **OK**. The Web page will appear in the content frame.

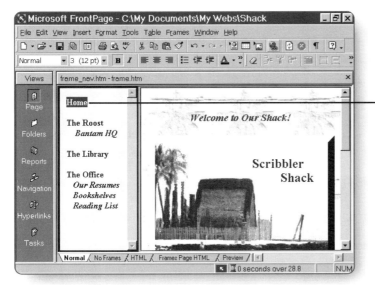

Linking Web Pages to the Content Frame

1. Select an **item** in the navigation frame that will link to a Web page in the content frame. The item will be highlighted.

2. Click on the **Hyperlink button**. The Create Hyperlink dialog box will open.

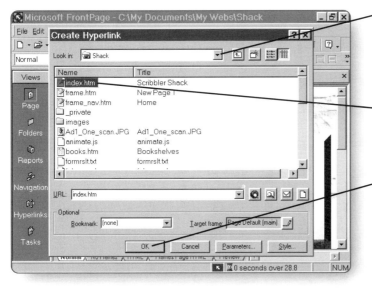

3. Click on the **folder** containing the page to which you want to create the hyperlink. The folder will be selected.

4. Click on the **page** to which you want to create the link. The file will be selected.

5. Click on **OK**. The link to the page will be created.

NOTE
Save your changes!

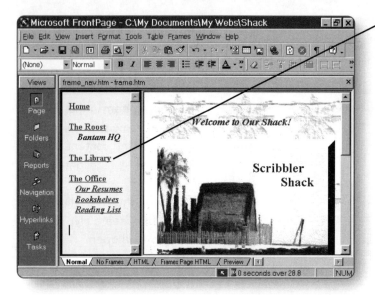

6. Create hyperlinks for each item in the navigation frame.

7. Click on the **Preview in Browser button**. Your default Web browser will appear and you will be able to test your frames page.

8. Click on a **hyperlink** in the navigation frame. The corresponding Web page will appear in the content frame.

Making Changes to the Frame Page

After previewing your frames page, you may decide that you want to change the size or appearance of individual frames in the frames page. Here are a few cosmetic enhancements that you can make to the frames page.

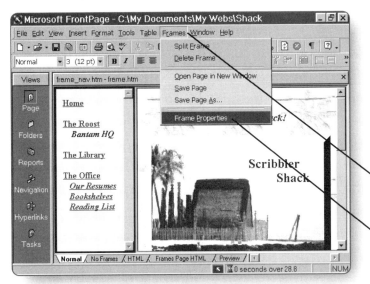

Changing Frame Spacing and Borders

1. Click on the **frame** that you want to change. The frame will be selected.

2. Click on **Frames**. The Frames menu will appear.

3. Click on **Frame Properties**. The Frame Properties dialog box will open.

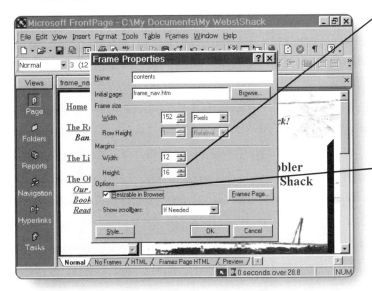

4. Click on the **up and down arrows** to the right of the Margins text boxes. This will increase or decrease the number of pixels between the frame and the text contained within the frame.

5. Click on the **Resizable in Browser check box.** If you don't want to give your visitors the ability to resize the frames in a browser window, the check box should be blank.

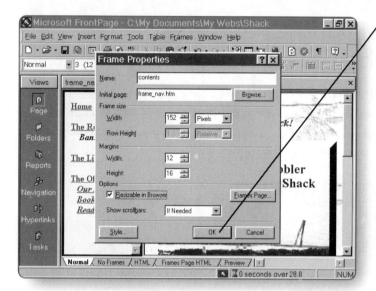

6. Click on **OK**. Your changes will be made.

TIP

So that your visitors can see all of a Web page, you'll want to display a scroll bar when needed. Click on the down arrow next to the Show scrollbars list box and select the If Needed option.

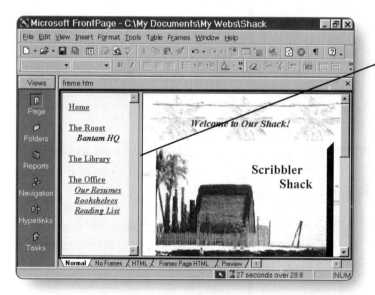

Resizing a Frame

1. Click and hold the **mouse button** on the border between the frames. The mouse pointer will change to a double arrow.

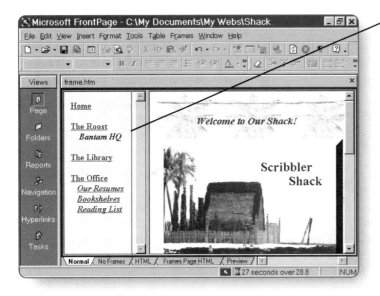

2. Drag the **mouse pointer** in either direction. The frames will change size.

3. Release the **mouse button** when the frames are the desired size.

Adding and Deleting Frames

After your frames page has been created, it's still easy to add and delete frames.

Adding Frames

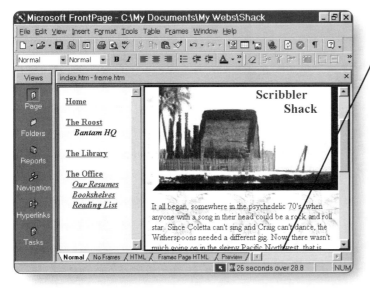

1. Place the **mouse pointer** next to the frame border where you want to create the new frame. The mouse pointer will change to a double arrow.

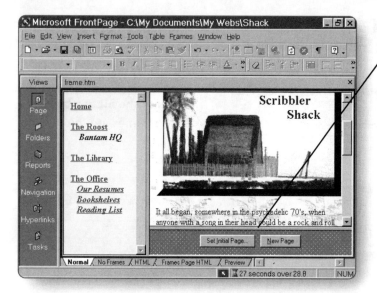

2. **Press and hold** the **Ctrl key.**

3. **Click and hold** the **mouse button** and **drag** the **mouse pointer** away from the area where you want the new frame created. A new frame will appear.

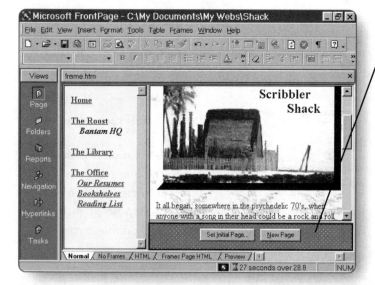

Deleting Frames

1. **Click** on the **frame** that you want to delete. The frame will be selected.

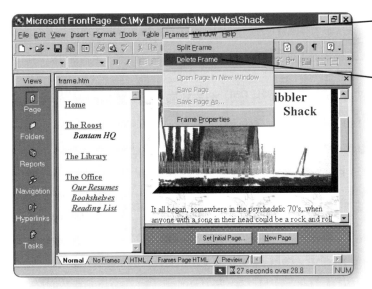

2. Click on **Frames**. The Frames menu will appear.

3. Click on **Delete Frame**. The frame will be deleted.

Part IV Review Questions

1. Where can you find pictures that you can use on your Web pages? *See "Inserting Images" in Chapter 9.*

2. What are three effects that you can apply to your images to make them look different? *See "Editing Images" in Chapter 10.*

3. What are the different shapes that you can use to create hotspots on image maps? *See "Designing Image Maps" in Chapter 10.*

4. Does FrontPage give you the ability to use your own images to create hover buttons? *See "Using Hover Buttons" in Chapter 11.*

5. How can you create a slideshow on a Web page? *See "Creating Banners" in Chapter 11.*

6. What are the ways that you can make text move around on a Web page? *See "Adding a Marquee" in Chapter 11.*

7. What are some of the form templates included with FrontPage? *See "Creating the Form" in Chapter 12.*

8. If you want to conserve space on your Web page, what is the best type of form field to use? *See "Creating Drop-Down Lists" in Chapter 12.*

9. Does the Themes feature of FrontPage work when building a frames page? *See "Creating the Frames Page" in Chapter 13.*

10. What is the easiest way to add a new frame to an existing frames page? *See "Adding and Deleting Frames" in Chapter 13.*

PART V

Finishing Your Web Site

14

Updating Your Web Site

Hopefully, you've been having fun creating your Web site. Has your Web grown from a few pages and just two levels to a dozen pages on three levels? Is there also a collection of images and other multimedia elements that have found their way onto the pages? Have you glanced at your filing system lately? Many tend to ignore the stacks of files that pile up on the computer, but managing your files doesn't have to be such a chore. FrontPage uses the same easy-to-use file management system found in other Windows programs. It also does some of your site management tasks for you. In this chapter, you'll learn how to:

- Keep all your hyperlinks in good working order
- Manage the files used to create your Web site
- Create a to-do list to keep your Web project organized

Verifying Hyperlinks

During your Web travels, you've probably clicked on a hyperlink that lead you nowhere. If you're a good netizen (net citizen), maybe you sent the Web master a message letting him or her know of the broken link. Or maybe you just moved on. There is something you can do to make sure this doesn't happen at your Web site. The following sections will show you how to find and repair broken hyperlinks.

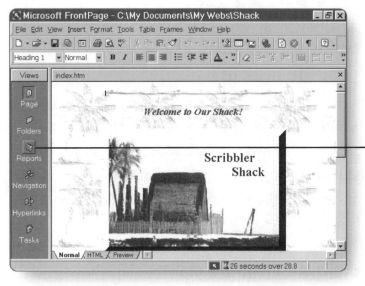

Checking All the Hyperlinks in a Web

1. Save any **changes** that you may have made on all open pages.

2. Click on the **Reports button** in the Views bar. The Site Summary will appear.

NOTE

Before you can begin checking your hyperlinks, you'll need to connect to the Internet.

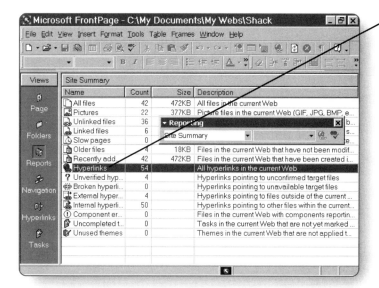

3. Double-click on the **Hyperlinks report**. The Broken Hyperlinks report will appear.

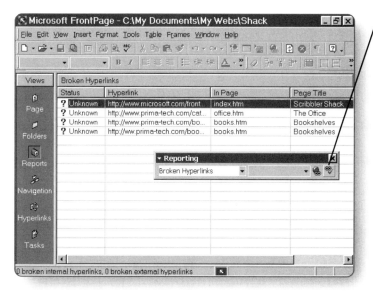

4. Click on the **Verify Hyperlinks button** on the Reporting toolbar. The Verify Hyperlinks dialog box will open and will already be set up to verify all the hyperlinks in your Web site.

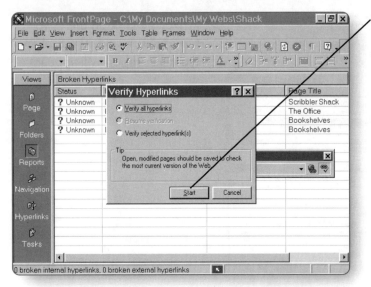

5. Click on **Start**. FrontPage will begin verifying each hyperlink in your Web site.

As FrontPage works down the list of hyperlinks, you can watch the validation progress. The following symbols indicate the status of each hyperlink:

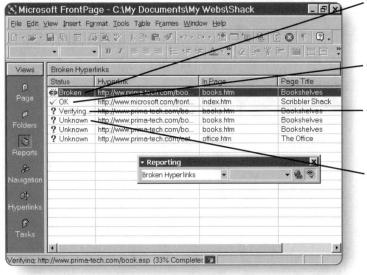

- **Broken** shows that the hyperlink does not connect to a valid URL address.

- **OK** shows that the hyperlink works correctly.

- **Verifying** shows that FrontPage is currently verifying the hyperlink.

- **Unknown** shows that FrontPage was unable to determine the status of the hyperlink, or has not checked that address yet.

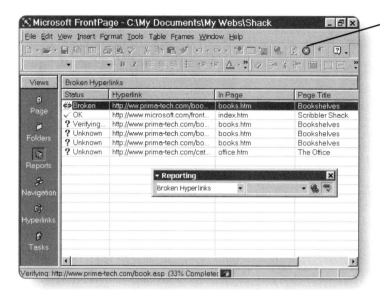

6. Click on the **Stop button** on the Standard toolbar. FrontPage will stop verifying the status of the hyperlinks.

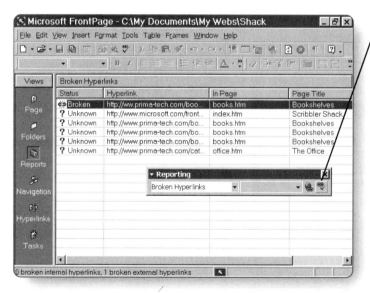

7. Click on the **Verify Hyperlinks button**. The Verify Hyperlinks dialog box will open with the Resume verification option button selected.

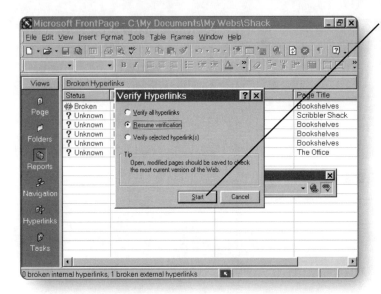

8. Click on the **Start button**. FrontPage will resume verifying the status of all the hyperlinks.

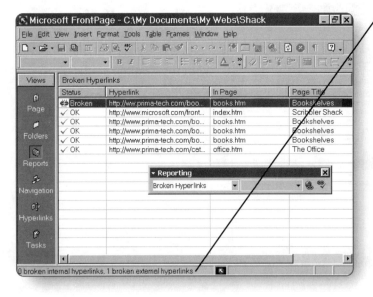

When the verification process is complete, the Status bar lets you know how many external and internal hyperlinks are broken.

NOTE

When you close FrontPage, the program does not store information collected about the status of hyperlinks.

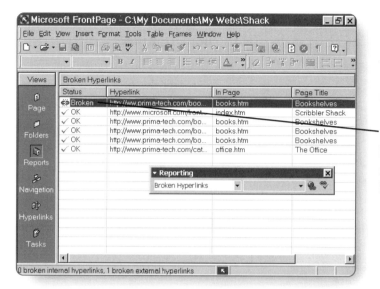

Fixing Hyperlinks

Any hyperlink that displays a broken status will need to be repaired.

1. Double-click on the **broken hyperlink** that you want to repair. The Edit Hyperlink dialog box will open.

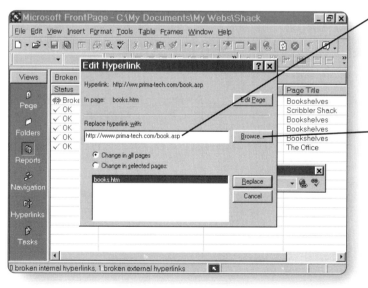

2. Type the **correct URL** for the hyperlink in the Replace hyperlink with text box.

TIP

If you click on the Browse button, your default Web browser will open and you can look for the correct address. When you have found the correct address, close the browser and the URL address will appear in the Replace hyperlink with text box.

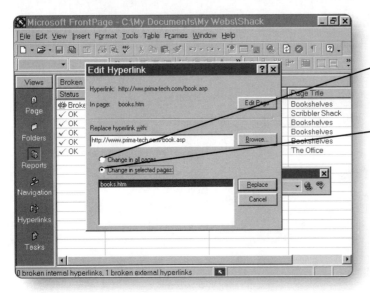

3. Choose one of the following **option buttons**:

- **Change in all pages** will repair the broken hyperlink in every place that it appears.

- **Change in selected pages** will repair the broken hyperlink only on selected pages. Click on this option button, then click on the pages in which you want the hyperlink fixed.

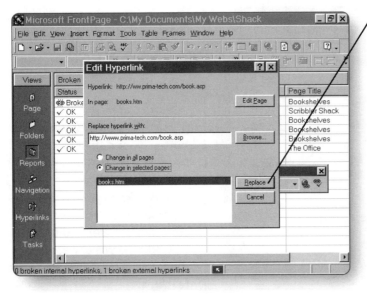

4. Click on **Replace**. The status of the hyperlink will change to Unknown.

NOTE

If you are still connected to the Internet, the status of the hyperlink will be verified. If you aren't connected, you may want to re-verify the hyperlink status at a later time.

Managing Files

Two different views in FrontPage allow you to manage your files: the Folders view and the Navigation view. You'll find that working in these two views feels somewhat like working in Windows Explorer. For routine maintenance, you may find it easiest to work in the Folders view.

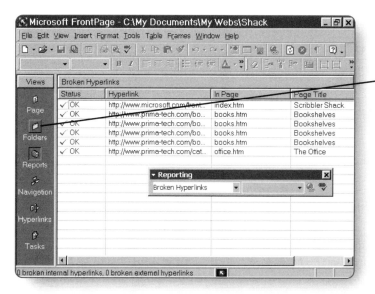

Sorting through Your Files

1. Click on the **Folders view button**. The Folders view window will appear.

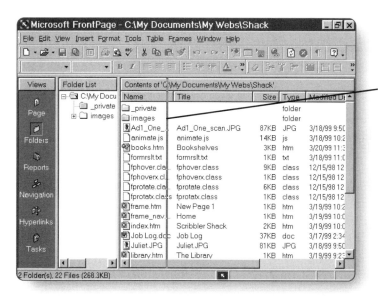

2. Change the **viewing area** using any of the following methods:

- Change the frame size by placing the mouse pointer over the frame border, click and hold the mouse button, drag the frame border to the desired position, and release the mouse button.

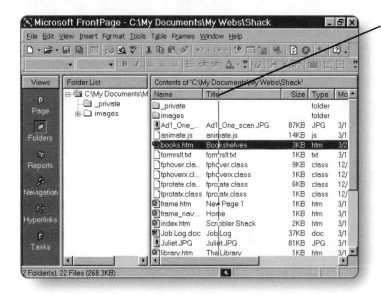

- Change the column size by placing the mouse pointer between the two column headings, click and hold the mouse button, drag the column border to the desired position, and release the mouse button.

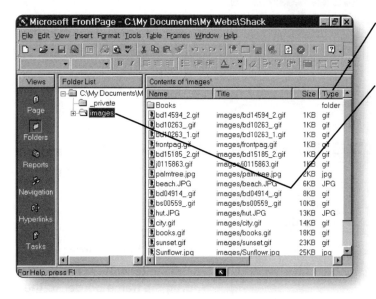

- Sort entries within a column by clicking on the column header.

- View the content of a folder by clicking on the folder.

Organizing Your Filing System

The easiest way to organize your files is to create folders and move groups of files that belong together into these folders.

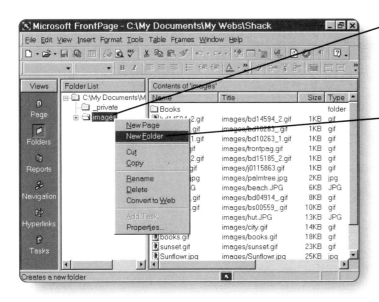

1. Right-click on the **folder** within which you want to create the new folder. A menu will appear.

2. Click on **New Folder**. The New Folder icon will appear in the Contents list.

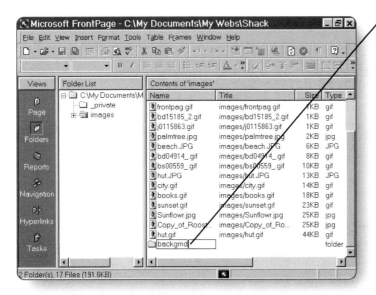

3. Type a **name** for the folder. The folder name will replace the "New Folder" text.

4. Press Enter. The new folder will be created. Now you can begin moving files to the new folder.

TIP

To see the subfolders contained within a folder, click on the plus sign next to the folder.

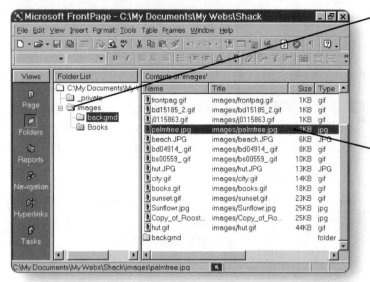

5. In the Folder List, **click** on the **folder** that contains the file you want to move. The folder will be selected and its list of files will display in the Contents window.

6. In the Contents window, **click and hold** on the **file** that you want to move. The file will be selected and the mouse pointer will have a gray box attached to it.

7. Drag the **mouse pointer** to the folder where you want to place the file and release the mouse button. The Rename dialog box will appear.

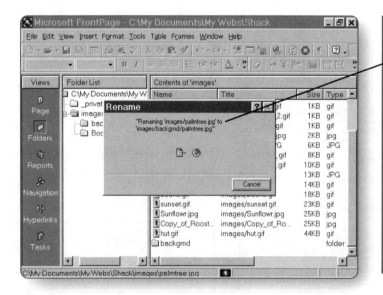

NOTE

When you move a file in this way, FrontPage automatically changes any internal hyperlinks associated with that file. You don't need to edit these hyperlinks manually. When FrontPage has finished recalculating all the hyperlinks associated with the file, the file appears in its new folder.

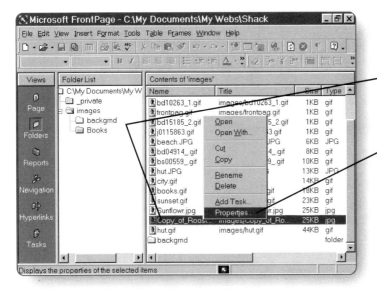

Viewing File Attributes

1. **Right-click** on the **file** that has attributes you want to view. A shortcut menu will appear.

2. **Click** on **Properties**. The Properties dialog box will appear with the General tab displayed.

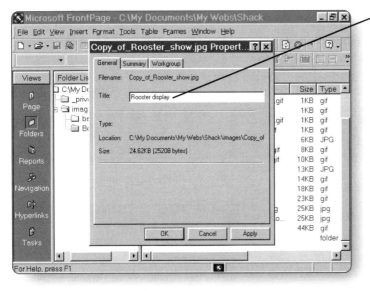

3. **Type** a new **title** for the file in the Title text box, if desired.

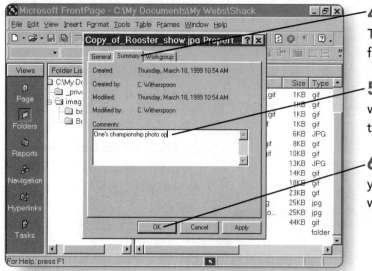

4. **Click** on the **Summary tab**. The Summary tab will come forward.

5. **Type** any **comments** you want to save about the file in the Comments text box.

6. **Click** on **OK**. The changes you make to the file's properties will be applied.

Working with the Tasks List

While you have been working on your Web pages, you may have noticed that some of the FrontPage dialog boxes contain a button or an option that allows you to add a task. This feature creates a to-do list that will help you keep track of work that needs to be done. With this task list, you can assign a priority or delegate a task.

Adding Tasks When Adding a New Page

1 **Click** on the **Page view button** in the Views bar. The Page view will appear.

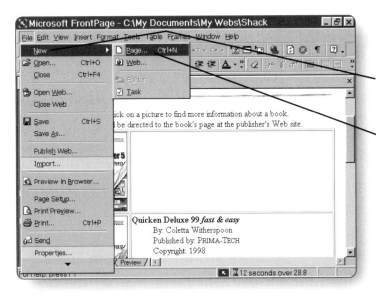

2. Click on **File**. The File menu will appear.

3. Click on **New**. A second menu will appear.

4. Click on **Page**. The New dialog box will appear with the General tab displayed.

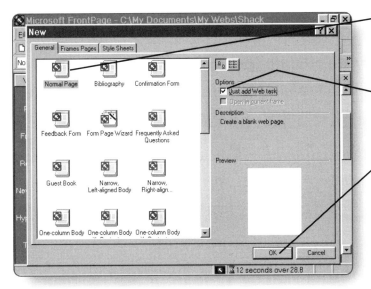

5. Click on the type of **page** that you want to create. The page template will be selected.

6. Click on **Just add Web task**. A check mark will appear in the box.

7. Click on **OK**. The Save As dialog box will appear.

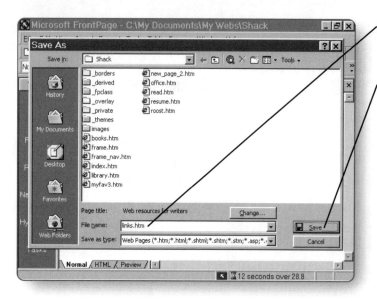

8. **Type** a **file name** for the Web page.

9. **Click** on **Save**. The new page will appear only as a task in the Task List.

TIP

To change the title of the page, click on the Change button.

Adding Tasks During a Spell Check

1. **Click** on the **Navigation view button**. The Navigation view will appear.

2. **Click** on the **Spelling button**. The Spelling dialog box will open.

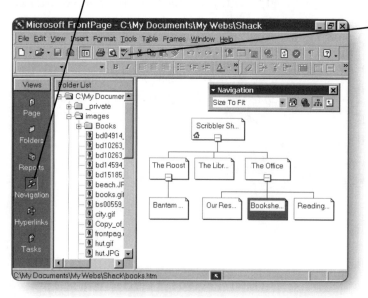

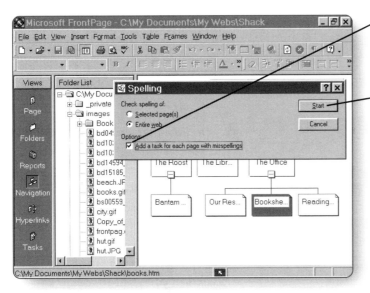

3. Click on **Add a task for each page with misspellings**. A check mark will appear in the box.

4. Click on **Start**. The spell check will check each page for misspelled words and add a task to the list for each page that contains misspellings.

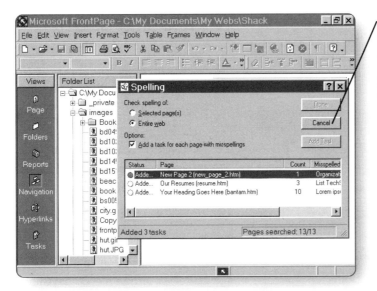

5. Click on the **Cancel button**. The tasks will be added to the Task List and will be waiting for you when you want to tackle this job.

Creating a New Task

There may be times where you will want to add a task without first having to perform some action (such as creating a new page or spell checking). For example, you may want to remind yourself to do some research on a topic that you are covering in your Web site. You may want to make some changes to an image you added to a page. You can add these reminders to the Task List.

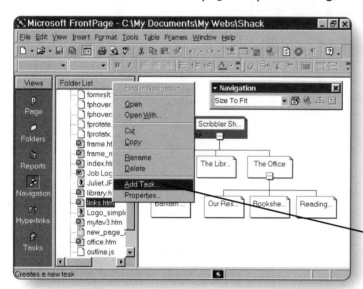

1. **Right-click** on the **file** to which you want to assign a task. A shortcut menu will appear.

2. **Click** on **Add Task**. The New Task dialog box will open.

3. **Type** a descriptive **title** for the task in the Task name text box.

4. **Click** on an **option button** to select the priority to be given to the task. The option will be selected.

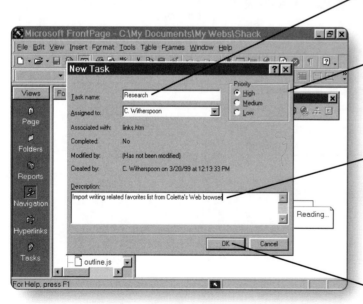

5. **Type** a **description** of the problem, the steps needed to be taken on the file, or anything else that will remind you how to handle the task in the Description text box.

6. **Click** on **OK**. The new task will be added to the Tasks List.

Completing Tasks

Now that you've given yourself all this work to do, it's time to see what is listed and get some of it done.

1. Click on the **Tasks view button**. The Tasks list will appear.

2. Right-click on the **task** on which you want to work. A shortcut menu will appear.

3. Click on **Start Task**. If you selected a task to create a new page, the new page will appear in the Page view window.

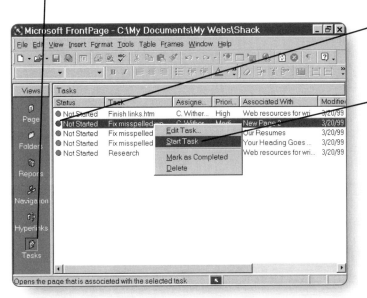

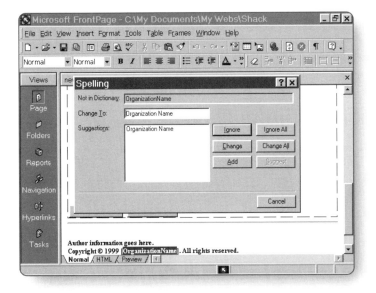

NOTE

If you added a task to fix misspelled words at a later time, the selected page will open and the Spelling dialog box will appear. You can fix any misspelling from this dialog box.

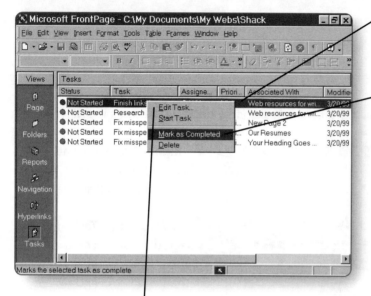

4. Right-click on the **task** that you just completed. A shortcut menu will appear.

5. Click on **Mark as Completed**. The task will be shown as completed in the Status column.

TIP

If you want to make changes to any item in the Tasks List, right-click on the item and select Edit Task. The Task Details dialog box will appear and you can make the necessary changes.

15

Publishing Your Web Site

You've just spent days, maybe weeks, building your Web site and making sure it works exactly the way you want. You've done a great job, so give yourself a pat on the back. You're now ready to publish your Web site so that the whole world can see your work. In this chapter, you'll learn how to:

- Find an ISP on whose server you can publish your Web site
- Use FrontPage or the Web Publishing Wizard to publish your Web site

Deciding Where to Publish Your Web Site

If you don't have an ISP, or if your ISP doesn't provide space on its server to publish your Web site, you can use one of the ISPs (Microsoft calls them Web Presence Providers) that has made a special arrangement with Microsoft to host Web sites for FrontPage users. Before you can look for an ISP, you'll need to be connected to the Internet.

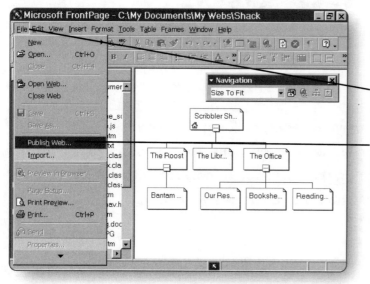

1. Open the **Web site** that you want to publish. The Web will appear in the window.

2. Click on **File**. The File menu will appear.

3. Click on **Publish Web**. The Publish Web dialog box will open.

NOTE

Before you can publish your Web site, you'll need to connect to the Internet.

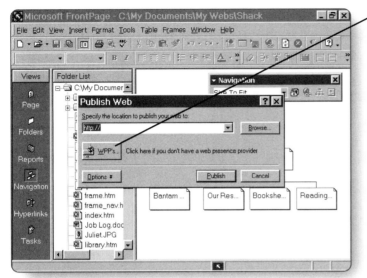

4. Click on the **WPP's button**. Your default Web browser will open, and the WPPs for FrontPage 2000 Web site will appear in the browser window.

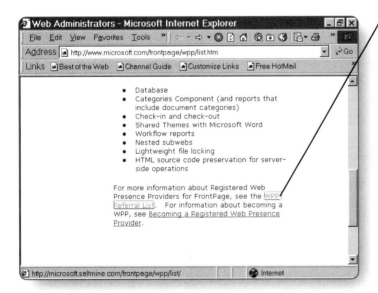

5. Scroll down the page and **click** on the **WPP Referral List hyperlink**. The WPP List page will appear.

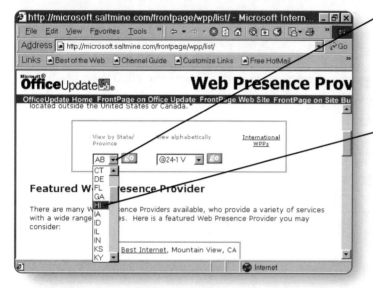

6. Click on the **down arrow** next to the View by State/ Province search area. A list of states (shown by their two letter abbreviation) will appear.

7. Click on your **state**. The state will be selected.

8. Click on the **Go hyperlink**. A list of Web Presence Providers in your state will appear in the browser window.

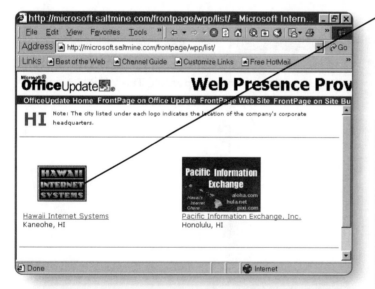

9. Click on the **hyperlink** for a Web Presence Provider. The FrontPage hosting page for the Web Presence Provider will appear in the Browser window.

NOTE

Each of the Web Presence Providers lists its prices and services on its respective FrontPage hosting page. If you don't feel that this Web Presence Provider will suit your needs, click on your browser's Back button and look for another provider. You don't have to use a provider on the Microsoft list; you can choose your own.

Getting on the Web

There are two methods that you can use to publish your Web site to the Internet. The first method is the easiest: let FrontPage do it for you. This method only works if the Web server to which you are publishing supports the FrontPage Server Extensions. If your ISP does not support the FrontPage Server Extensions (you may have to call your ISP and ask the technical support personnel), you will have to use the Web Publishing Wizard.

Letting FrontPage Do It For You

NOTE

Before you start publishing your Web site, make sure you are connected to the Internet.

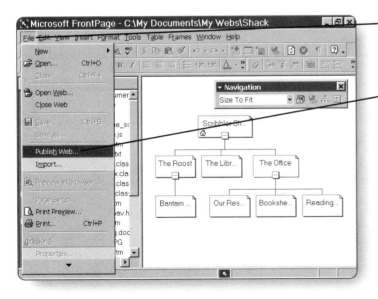

1. If the Publish Web dialog box is not open, **click** on **File**. The File menu will appear.

2. **Click** on **Publish Web**. The Publish Web dialog box will open.

NOTE

If the Publish FrontPage Web dialog box is still displayed on your screen after you search through the list of Web Presence Providers at the Microsoft Web site, you will need to skip steps 1 and 2.

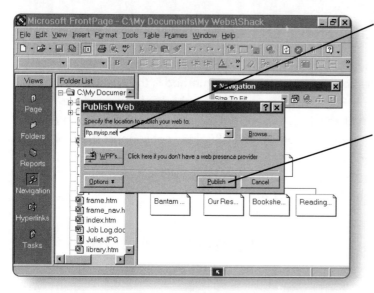

3. In the Specify the location to publish your web to text box, **type** the **host name** of the provider to whose server you want to publish your Web site.

4. Click on **Publish**. A download dialog box will open.

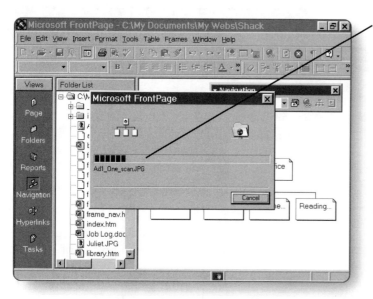

5. The status of the download will display in the dialog box. A confirmation dialog box will appear when the download is complete.

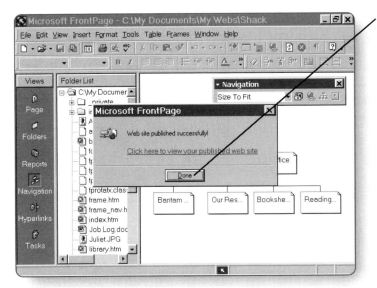

6. **Click** on **Done**. Your site will be placed on the Web.

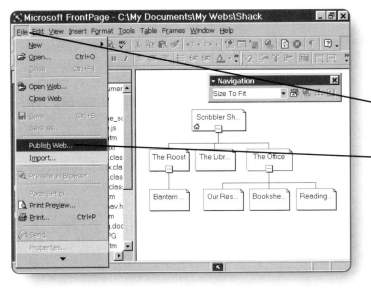

Using the FTP Wizard to Publish Your Web Site

1. **Click** on **File**. The File menu will appear.

2. **Click** on **Publish Web**. The Publish Web dialog box will open.

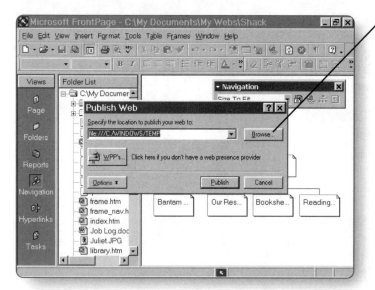

3. Click on the **Browse button**. The Open Web dialog box will open.

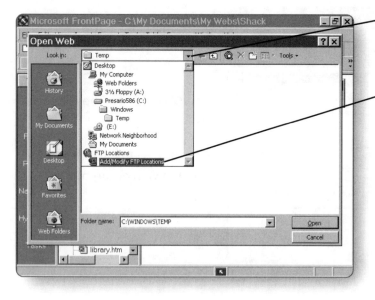

4. Click on the **down arrow** next to the Look in list box. A List of directories will appear.

5. Click on **Add/Modify FTP Locations**. The Add/Modify FTP Locations dialog box will open.

6. **Click** in the **Name of FTP site text box** and **type** the **FTP address** that your service provider specified for publishing your Web site.

7. **Click** on the **User option button**. The option will be selected and you will be able to enter your User ID and Password to access the FTP site.

8. **Click** in the **User text box** and **type** your **User ID** required by your service provider to access your Web space.

9. **Click** in the **Password text box** and type your password.

10. **Click** on **Add**. The FTP site will be added to the FTP Sites list.

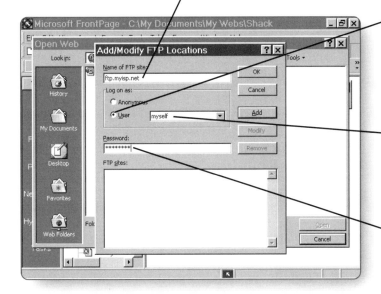

11. **Click** on **OK**. The ftp site will be added to the list in the Open Web dialog box.

NOTE

Check with your ISP for any special instructions before you publish your Web site.

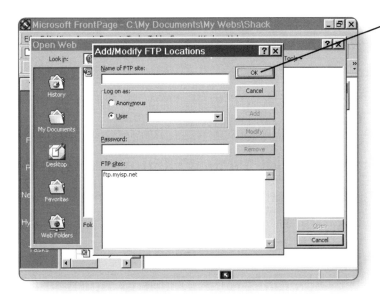

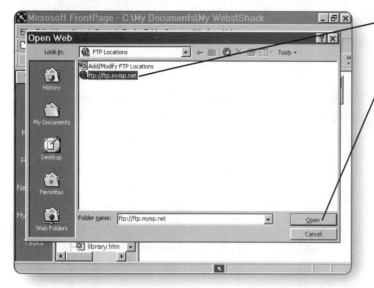

12. Click on the **FTP location** you just created. The FTP location will be selected.

13. Click on **Open**. The Publish Web dialog box will open.

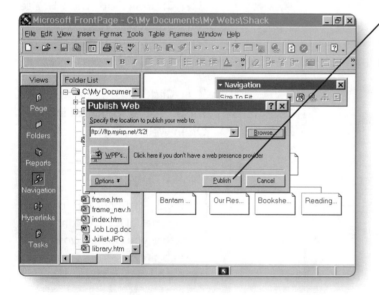

14. Click on **Publish**. The Name and Password Required dialog box will open.

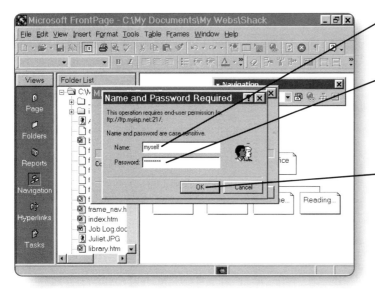

15. **Click** in the **Name text box** and type your User name.

16. **Click** in the **Password text box** and type the password needed to access the service provider's FTP site.

17. **Click** on **OK**. A download status dialog box will appear.

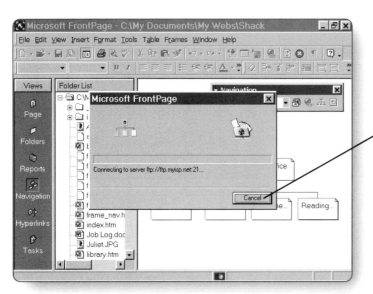

Your Web site will begin uploading to your ISP's Web Server. When the upload is complete, a confirmation dialog box will open.

18. If you wish to cancel the transfer, **click** on **Cancel**. When the upload is complete, a confirmation dialog box will open.

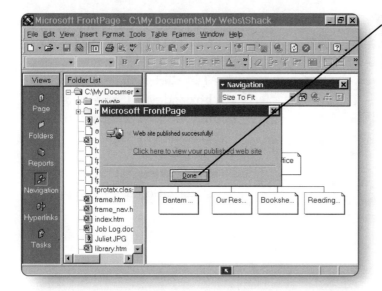

19. Click on **Done**. You're on the Web! Have a great time and keep those pages updated.

Part V Review Questions

1. How can you use FrontPage to verify that the hyperlinks in your Web pages work correctly? *See "Verifying Hyperlinks" in Chapter 14.*

2. How do you sort a list of files? *See "Managing Files" in Chapter 14.*

3. How do you create a new folder? *See "Managing Files" in Chapter 14.*

4. How can you tell if a task can be added to the Task List so that you can be reminded to work on it later? *See "Working with the Tasks List" in Chapter 14.*

5. In what two places can you create a new task? *See "Working with the Tasks List" in Chapter 14.*

6. How do you find a good spot to publish your Web site? *See "Deciding Where to Publish Your Web Site" in Chapter 15.*

7. Is it required that you use a Microsoft sponsored provider to publish your Web site? *See "Deciding Where to Publish Your Web Site" in Chapter 15.*

8. What are the two different methods that FrontPage uses to publish your Web site to a Web server? *See "Getting on the Web" in Chapter 15.*

9. How do you use the FTP feature of FrontPage to publish your Web site? *See "Using the FTP Wizard to Publish Your Web Site" in Chapter 15.*

10. Where can you look to see how much of your Web site has downloaded to the Web server? *See "Getting on the Web" in Chapter 15.*

PART VI

Appendixes

A

Office 2000 Installation

Installing Office 2000 is typically very quick and easy. In this appendix, you'll learn how to:

- Install Office 2000 on your computer
- Choose which Office components you want to install
- Detect and repair problems
- Reinstall Office
- Add and remove components
- Uninstall Office 2000 completely
- Install content from other Office CDs

Installing the Software

The installation program for the Office 2000 programs is automatic. In most cases, you can simply follow the instructions onscreen.

> **NOTE**
>
> When you insert the Office 2000 CD for the first time, you may see a message that the installer has been updated, prompting you to restart your system. Do so, and when you return to Windows after restarting, remove the CD and reinsert it so that the Setup program starts up automatically again.

1. Insert the **Office 2000 CD-ROM** into your computer's CD-ROM drive. The Windows Installer will start and the Customer Information dialog box will open.

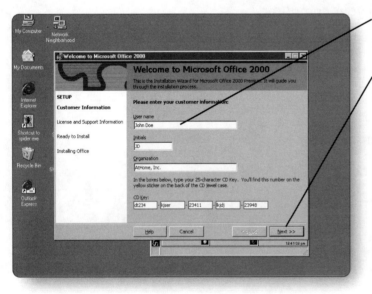

2. Type all of the **information** requested.

3. Click on **Next**. The End User License Agreement will appear.

> **NOTE**
>
> You'll find the CD Key number on a sticker on the back of the Office CD jewel case.

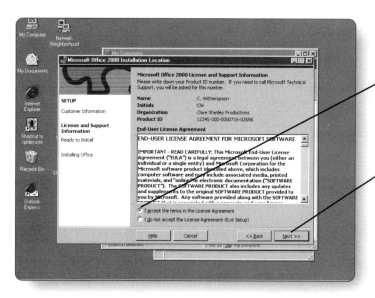

4. Read the **License Agreement**.

5. Click on the **I accept the terms in the License Agreement option button**. The option will be selected.

6. Click on **Next**. The Ready To Install dialog box will open.

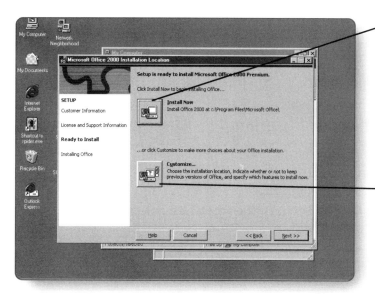

7a. Click on the **Install Now button.** Use this option to install Office on your computer with the default settings. This is the recommended installation for most users.

OR

7b. Click on the **Customize button**, if you want to choose which components to install or where to install them. The Installation Location dialog box will open. Then see the next section, "Choosing Components," for guidance.

8. Wait while the **Office software** installs on your computer. When the setup has completed, the Installer Information box will open.

9. **Click** on **Yes**. The Setup Wizard will restart your computer. After your computer has restarted, Windows will update your system settings and then finish the Office installation and configuration process.

Choosing Components

If you selected option 7b in the previous section, you have the choice of installing many different programs and components.

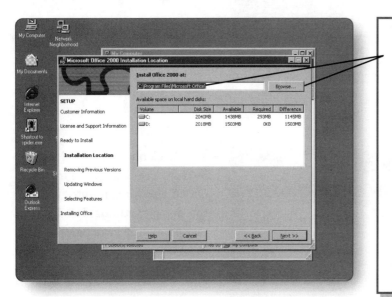

NOTE

For a custom installation, you have the option of placing Office in a different location on your computer. It is recommended that you use the default installation location. If you want to install Office in a different directory, type the directory path in the text box or click on the Browse button to select a directory.

1. **Click** on **Next**. The Selecting Features dialog box will open.

2. **Click** on a **plus sign (+)** to expand a list of features. The features listed under the category will appear.

3. **Click** on the **down arrow (▼)** to the right of the hard drive icon. A menu of available installation options for the feature will appear.

4. **Click** on the **button** next to the individual option, and choose a setting for that option:

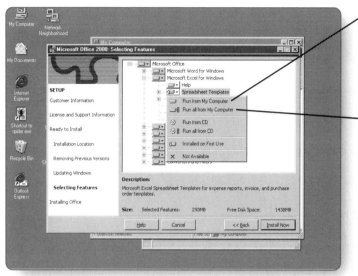

- **Run from My Computer**. The component will be fully installed, so that you will not need the Office CD in the CD-ROM drive to use it.

- **Run all from My Computer**. The selected component and all the components subordinate to it will be fully installed.

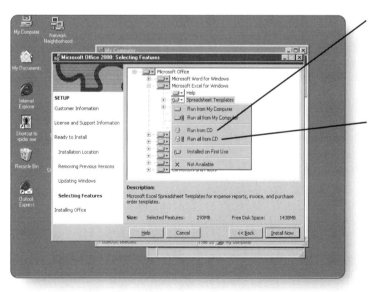

- **Run from CD**. The component will be installed, but you will need to have the Office CD in the CD-ROM drive to use it.

- **Run all from CD**. The selected component and all the components subordinate to it will need to have the Office CD in the CD-ROM drive to use it.

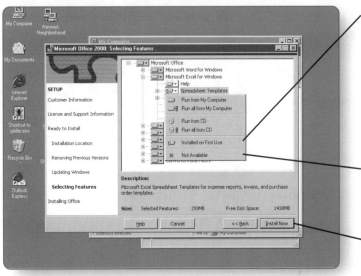

● **Installed on First Use**. The first time you try to activate the component, you will be prompted to insert the Office CD to fully install it. This is good for components that you are not sure whether you will need or not.

● **Not Available**. The component will not be installed at all.

5. Click on **Install Now**. The Installing dialog box will open.

In a Custom installation, you'll be asked whether you want to update Internet Explorer to version 5.0. Your choices are:

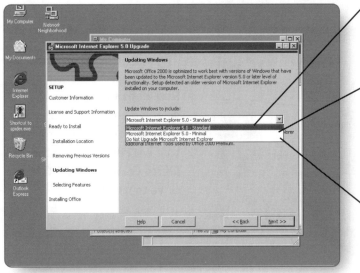

● **Microsoft Internet Explorer 5.0—Standard**. This is the default, and the right choice for most people.

● **Microsoft Internet Explorer 5.0—Minimal**. This is the right choice if you are running out of hard disk space but still would like to use Internet Explorer 5.0.

● **Do Not Upgrade Microsoft Internet Explorer**. Use this if you don't want Internet Explorer (for example, if you always use another browser such as Netscape Navigator, or if you have been directed by your system administrator not to install Internet Explorer 5).

Working with Maintenance Mode

Maintenance Mode is a feature of the Setup program. Whenever you run the Setup program again, after the initial installation, Maintenance Mode starts automatically. It enables you to add or remove features, repair your Office installation (for example, if files have become corrupted), and remove Office completely. There are several ways to rerun the Setup program (and thus enter Maintenance Mode):

- Reinsert the Office 2000 CD. The Setup program may start automatically.

- If the Setup program does not start automatically, double-click on the CD icon in the My Computer window.

- If double-clicking on the CD icon doesn't work, right-click on the CD icon and click on Open from the shortcut menu. Then double-click on the Setup.exe file in the list of files that appears.

- From the Control Panel in Windows, click on the Add/ Remove Programs button. Then on the Install/Uninstall tab, click on Microsoft Office 2000 in the list, and finally, click on the Add/Remove button.

After entering Maintenance Mode, choose the button for the activity you want. Each option is briefly described in the following sections.

Repairing or Reinstalling Office

If an Office program is behaving strangely, or refuses to work, chances are good that a needed file has become corrupted. But which file? You have no way of knowing, so you can't fix the problem yourself.

If this happens, you can either repair Office or completely reinstall it. Both options are accessed from the Repair Office button in Maintenance Mode.

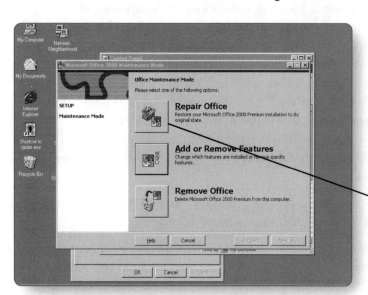

1. Click on the **Repair Office button** in Maintenance Mode.

2a. Click on **Reinstall Office** to repeat the last installation.

OR

2b. Click on **Repair errors in my Office installation** to simply fix what's already in place.

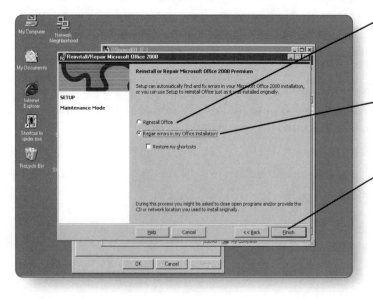

3. Click on **Finish**. The process will start.

> **TIP**
>
> You can also repair individual Office programs by opening the Help menu in each program and clicking on Detect and Repair. This works well if you are sure that one certain program is causing the problem, and it's quicker than asking the Setup program to check all of the installed programs.

Adding and Removing Components

Adding and removing components works just like selecting the components initially.

1. Click on the **Add or Remove Features button** in Maintenance Mode. The Update Features window will appear. This window works exactly the same as the window you saw in the "Choosing Components" section earlier in this appendix.

> **NOTE**
>
> Some features will attempt to automatically install themselves as you are working. If you have set a feature to be installed on first use, attempt to access that feature. You will be prompted to insert your Office 2000 CD, and the feature will be installed without further prompting.

Removing Office from Your PC

In the unlikely event that you should need to remove Office from your PC completely, click on Remove Office from the Maintenance Mode screen. Then follow the prompts to remove it from your system.

After removing Office, you will probably have a few remnants left behind that the Uninstall routine didn't catch. For example, there will probably still be a Microsoft Office folder in your Program Files folder or wherever you installed the program. You can delete that folder yourself.

CAUTION

If you plan to reinstall Office later, and you have created any custom templates, toolbars, or other items, you may want to leave the Microsoft Office folder alone, so that those items will be available to you after you reinstall.

Installing Content from Other Office CDs

Depending on the version of Office you bought, you may have more than one CD in your package. CD 1 contains all the basic Office components, such as Word, Outlook, PowerPoint, Excel, Access, and Internet Explorer. It may be the only CD you need to use.

The other CDs contain extra applications that come with the specific version of Office you purchased. They may include Publisher, FrontPage, a language pack, or a programmer and developer resource kit. Each of these discs has its own separate installation program.

The additional CDs should start their Setup programs automatically when you insert the disk in your drive. If not, browse the CD's content in My Computer or Windows Explorer and double-click on the Setup.exe file that you find on it.

B

Using Keyboard Shortcuts

You may have noticed the keyboard shortcuts listed on the right side of several of the menus. You can use these shortcuts to execute commands without using the mouse to activate menus. You may want to memorize these keyboard shortcuts. Not only will they speed your productivity, but they will also help decrease wrist strain caused by excessive mouse usage. In this appendix, you'll learn how to:

- Get up to speed with frequently used keyboard shortcuts
- Use keyboard combinations to edit text

Learning the Most Popular Shortcuts

Trying to memorize all these keyboard shortcuts isn't as hard as you may think. Windows applications all share the same keyboard combinations to execute common commands. Once you get accustomed to using some of these keyboard shortcuts in FrontPage, try them out on some of the other Microsoft Office programs.

Getting Help

You don't need to wade through menus to get some help using the program. Try these useful keyboard shortcuts.

To execute this command	Do this
Use FrontPage Help	Press the F1 key
Use the What's This? Button	Press the Shift and F1 keys simultaneously (Shift+F1)

Wading Through Web Pages

The following table shows you a few of the more common keyboard shortcuts that you may want to use when working with pages.

To execute this command	Do this
Create a new Web page	Press the Ctrl and N keys simultaneously (Ctrl+N)
Open a different Web page	Press Ctrl+O
Switch between open Web pages	Press Ctrl+Tab
Save a Web page	Press Ctrl+S
Refresh a Web page	Press F5
Print a Web page	Press Ctrl+P
Preview a page in a Web browser	Press Ctrl+Shift+B
Close a Web page	Press Ctrl+F4

Working with Text

The easiest keyboard shortcuts to learn are those that manipulate text. Try your hand at selecting, editing, and formatting text using some of the commonly used text combinations.

Selecting Text

Before you can perform any editing and formatting task to the text in your Web pages, you'll need to select the text. This table shows you how to use keyboard combinations to select text. Before you begin, you'll need to move the cursor to the beginning of the text that you want to select.

To execute this command	Do this
Highlight the character to the right of the cursor	Press Shift+Right Arrow
Highlight the character to the left	Press Shift+Left Arrow
Highlight an entire word	Press Ctrl+Shift+Right Arrow
Highlight an entire line	Press Shift+End
Highlight a paragraph	Press Ctrl+Shift+ Down Arrow
Select an entire page	Press Ctrl+A

Editing Text

Once you have selected the text to which you want to make the editing changes, apply one of the combinations in the following table.

To execute this command	Do this
Delete the character to the left of the cursor	Press Backspace
Delete the character to the right	Press Delete
Delete the word to the left of the cursor	Press Ctrl+Backspace
Delete the word to the right	Press Ctrl+Delete
Delete selected text (or other Web page element) from a Web page	Press Ctrl+X
Make a copy of selected text	Press Ctrl+C
Paste the copied text	Press Ctrl+V
Spell check a Web page	Press the F7 key
Find text on Web pages	Press Ctrl+F
Replace text on Web pages	Press Ctrl+H
Undo an action	Press Ctrl+Z
Redo an action	Press Ctrl+Y

Formatting Text

To make your text look good, you may want to change the font, font style, or one of the many standardized paragraph styles.

To execute this command	Do this
Change the font	Press Ctrl+Shift+F
Change the size of the font	Press Ctrl+Shift+P
Make selected text bold	Press Ctrl+B
Make selected text italic	Press Ctrl+I
Center a paragraph on the Web page	Press Ctrl+E
Left align a paragraph	Press Ctrl+L
Right align a paragraph	Press Ctrl+R
Left indent a paragraph	Press Ctrl+M
Right indent a paragraph	Press Ctrl+Shift+M
Apply a style	Press Ctrl+Shift+S

Glossary

Active hyperlink. The currently selected hyperlink in a visitor's Web browser.

ActiveX control. A component of Dynamic HTML that allows you to add features such as animation, video, credit card transactions, or financial calculations on your Web pages.

Animated GIF. A graphic file that contains several images. When these images are viewed in a Web browser, they act much like a short video (or cartoon).

Aspect ratio. The relationship between the height and width of an image.

Banner. A graphical image that usually appears at the top of a Web page and contains pictures, the title of the page, or advertising.

Banner Ad Manager. A dynamic HTML element used in FrontPage to display a series of images in a slideshow fashion, often with transition effects between the images.

Bevel. An effect applied to an image that gives it the appearance of being inside a frame, much like a framed picture that you might find hanging on your office wall.

Bookmark. A specific place on a page to which you can point with a hyperlink. When your visitors click on a hyperlink to a bookmark, their Web browsers will take them to that particular place on the page, not just to the top of the page.

Broken hyperlink. A hyperlink that does not connect to another Web page.

Bullet list. A method of displaying an unordered list of items, in which each item is set off by a bullet character.

Cell. The box created by the intersection of a row and a column within a table.

Cell padding. The space between the cell border and the contents of the cell.

Cell spacing. The width of the cell borders, measured in pixels.

Channel. A method that allows visitors to a site to subscribe to the site so that they can view your Web pages offline and so that they will be informed when the site is updated.

Channel Definition Format. The type of file that makes it possible for visitors to view Web pages as a channel.

Clip Art. Images, video, and other graphics that can be included in your Web pages free of charge and without restriction.

Column. The vertical band of cells in a table.

Crop. To resize an image by deleting the outside edges. In FrontPage, images can only be cropped in a rectangular shape.

Desktop component. A small window that appears on the visitor's desktop when they subscribe to a Web site through a channel and sets up the channel for offline viewing.

Embedded files. All the image, sound, or video files that are contained in your Web pages.

External hyperlink. A link to a page that is not located within your Web.

Files pane. A window in FrontPage that displays the contents of your Web. The Files pane looks much like the list of files you see in Windows Explorer.

Folders view. Displays how the Web content is organized.

Form. A page that contains data fields that visitors to your Web site can fill in and send as e-mail and the results of which

you can store as a file contained in your Web or on the Web server.

Form field. A data entry field on a form page.

Format toolbar. A toolbar in FrontPage that allows you to quickly add styles (such as bold or centering) to text and paragraphs.

Forms toolbar. A toolbar in FrontPage that helps you to add form fields to a data form.

Frame. One of a number of separate windows that appear in the browser window. These windows are usually separated by a border and may contain scroll bars.

Frames page. The Web page that controls how the individual frames appear when viewed in a Web browser.

FrontPage Server Extensions. Software programs, stored on a Web server, that support some of the advanced features of FrontPage and allow these features to work correctly.

GIF. Graphics Interchange Format, a file format used for image files commonly found on the World Wide Web. GIF files are usually comprised of drawings created in a computer graphics program and contain less than 256 colors. GIF files are highly compressed so that they transmit quickly over the Internet.

Heading. A type of paragraph style that you can use to emphasize titles and intro-ductions in your Web pages. FrontPage supports six different heading styles.

Home page. The first page that appears by default in your visitors' Web browsers when they first access your Web site. Your home page is usually named "index.htm" or "default.htm."

Horizontal rule. A line image that is used to separate sections of text in your Web pages.

Hotspot. An area within an image map on which a visitor can click and be taken to another location within a Web site. An image map usually contains more than one hotspot.

Hover button. A navigational button on a Web page that becomes animated by either changing its color or image when the mouse pointer is placed over it.

HTML. Hypertext Markup Language. This is the programming language that is used to create Web pages. With FrontPage, you do not need to learn HTML. FrontPage creates all the HTML code for you.

Hyperlink. The method used to move from Web page to Web page. A hyperlink can be a word, a group of words, an image, or an image map. When a visitor clicks on one of the linked elements, the page that is linked to the hyperlink will appear in his or her Web browser.

Hyperlinks view. Displays the links within the pages of your Web site and the links to external pages on the Internet.

Image. A picture or graphics file that is included in a Web page. Most images are in the GIF or JPEG format.

Image bullet. A picture or graphic that is used in a bullet list in place of the standard black dot.

Image handles. When you click on an image in a page, small black boxes appear at the corners and sides of the image. When the image handles are activated, you can move or resize an image by clicking on them and dragging the mouse pointer.

Image map. A picture or graphic that contains several hotspots on which visitors can click to be taken to different parts of your Web site.

Image toolbar. A FrontPage toolbar that contains buttons to help you make changes to the way images appear on the Web page.

Initial page. The first page that displays in a frame window when the page opens in the browser.

Internal hyperlink. A link to a page, or to a certain spot on a page, that is found within your Web site.

Internet. A global network of computers that provides public communication services to individuals, businesses, and organizations. Services provided by the Internet include e-mail, FTP, and Web browsing. The World Wide Web is only one part of the Internet.

Internet Explorer. The Web browser developed by Microsoft Corporation.

Java. A programming language created by Sun Microsystems. Java is used to create small programs that can be run from within a Web browser.

Java applet. A small program created using the Java programming language. Java applets are downloaded to your computer from the Web site you are visiting. Your computer executes the program in your Web browser.

JPEG. Joint Photographic Experts Group, a file format used on the Internet to display photographic quality images. JPEG files are compressed so that they can be downloaded quickly to display in Web pages.

Mailto. A type of hyperlink that allows visitors to your Web site to send you an e-mail message. When visitors click on the mailto hyperlink, a new message window from their default e-mail program will open with your e-mail address already typed in the To area.

Marquee. An area on a Web page that displays text that scrolls across the page.

Navigation buttons. Graphical elements in a Web page that help direct your visitors to the different pages in your Web site.

Navigation view. Shows an organization chart of your Web site.

Nested list. A list that is a subset of the main list. Nested lists are normally indented from the main list.

One line text box. A form element that allows your visitors to type short amounts of information into a form.

Page. A single document within your Web site that contains text, graphics, hyperlinks, and other elements.

Page template. A predesigned page that you can use as a basis for other pages that you may want to create. A template contains standardized text, image placeholders, prebuilt tables, or any other elements that you may want to include in your Web pages.

Page title. The name of a particular Web page. The page title can appear in any of your Web banners and in the title bar of the Web browser used by visitors to your site.

Page View. A tool for creating, designing, and editing World Wide Web pages. You can add text, images, tables, and forms, and they will be displayed as they would appear in a Web browser. You do not need to learn HTML to produce these elements, because FrontPage creates all the HTML code for you.

Publish. To put your Web site on the Internet so that others can visit your Web site.

Radio button. A form element that a visitor clicks on to indicate his or her selection.

Resample. To change the size of a graphic image.

Row. A horizonal collection of cells in a table.

Scrolling text box. A form element that allows visitors to input large amounts of text in a form. The text box takes up a specified area in the form but does not limit the amount of information that can be input. Visitors can view their input by using the scroll bars.

Shared borders. An area that can be set up on several Web pages so that any content input into these shared areas will appear on all pages.

Size handle. When you click on an image in a page, small black boxes appear at the corners and sides of the image. You can click and hold on these handles while dragging the mouse pointer to resize an image.

Standard toolbar. A toolbar found in FrontPage that contains buttons to execute the most common menu commands.

Status bar. An area at the bottom of the FrontPage screen that displays information about the current task or about a command that you have selected.

Style. Shortcuts for formatting text. Styles also help keep the text on your Web pages uniform.

Table. A collection of cells arranged in rows and columns. Tables are used to display information in a neat and organized manner. They can also be used as page layout elements to help keep text and graphics where you want them on a page.

Table toolbar. A toolbar found in FrontPage that makes it quick and easy to create, edit, and format tables.

Task. An item that is placed in the FrontPage Tasks list. Also known as a "to-do" item.

Tasks view. Shows the finished and unfinished tasks that have been assigned to different parts of the Web.

Theme. A predesigned set of backgrounds, colors, images, navigation buttons, banners, and bullets. Themes are used to give your Web site a professional look. They also make it easy for you to get your Web site started.

Thumbnail. A thumbnail image is a small version of an image that contains a hyperlink to a full-size version of the same image.

Transition effect. An effect that occurs, such as fade-to-black, when a Web page is accessed or exited.

URL. Uniform Resource Locator. The URL provides the Internet address for a Web site.

Visited hyperlink. A hyperlink on a Web page that has already been accessed by the Web browser.

Washout. An effect applied to graphic images to give them a faded or sun-bleached look.

Web. A collection of linked Web pages that are stored on your computer or that have been published on a Web server.

Index

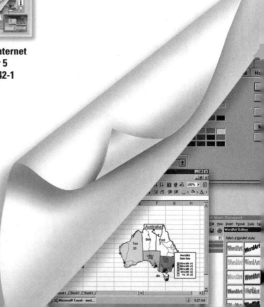